TELLING TWAIN

"Steve Daut is a master storyteller. His stories are humorous and interesting, sometime bordering on stand-up comedy. Specializing in Mark Twain stories, he captures the imagination as he brings out the wit and satire that made Mark Twain's stories loved by all."

—Beverly Black, storyteller

"Daut doesn't report from the sidelines—he leads readers into the heart of a story, pointing out keenly observed details with a slightly off kilter sense of humor."

—M.A. Engle, editor, *Community Observer*

"Steve Daut brings Mark Twain's clever humor and understanding of human nature into the 21st century with the feel of an earlier time in a way that is both accessible and enjoyable to modern readers and audiences."

—Laura Lee Hayes, storyteller and co-producer of
Story Night at Crazy Wisdom

"Steve Daut has always been a master of surprise and misdirection with a comfortingly informal, humorous tone. It's only natural that he decided to adapt Twain's works. He might not have realized it himself, but I think he's been setting himself up for "Telling Twain" his whole life."

—Brian Hamilton, former newspaper editor and publisher
and guest host at WUTC 88.1 radio, Chattanooga, TN

"I have had the pleasure of sharing several stages with Steve and would never hesitate to include his talent in a concert I was planning."

—Jane Fink, storyteller and producer

"I've been telling stories for over 30 years and yet, Steve's workshop gave me new ideas on how to focus and to improve my storytelling performance."

—Judy Sima, storyteller and coach

TELLING TWAIN

Modernized versions of Mark Twain's
best stories, with comments, historical
notes, and resources for storytellers,
teachers, and readers

Adapted by

Steve Daut

Parkhurst Brothers Publishers
MARION, MICHIGAN

www.parkhurstbrothers.com

Consumers may order Parkhurst Brothers books from their favorite online or bricks-and-mortar booksellers, expecting prompt delivery. Parkhurst Brothers books are distributed to the trade through the Chicago Distribution Center. Trade and library orders may be placed through Ingram Book Company, Baker & Taylor, Follett Library Resources, and other book industry wholesalers. To order from Chicago Distribution Center, phone 1-800-621-2736 or fax to 800-621-8476. Copies of this and other Parkhurst Brothers Publishers titles are available to organizations and corporations for purchase in quantity by contacting Special Sales Department at our home office location, listed on our website. Manuscript submission guidelines for this publishing company are available at our website.

Printed in the United States of America
First Edition, 2019
Printing history: 2019 2020 2021 2022   8 7 6 5 4 3 2 1

Cataloging in Publication Data: (2019)
1. Author--Daut, Steve 2. Humor-Americana 3. Twain, Mark--interpreted
p. cm.
818' 409 alk. paper

ISBN: Trade Paperback   978162491-132-3
ISBN: e-book   978162491- 133-0

Parkhurst Brothers Publishers believes that the universal study of history and the free and open exchange of ideas are essential for the maintenance of our freedoms. We support the First Amendment of the United States Constitution and encourage every citizen to study all sides of public policy questions, making up their own minds.

Cover art, cover design   Linda D. Parkhurst, Ph.D.
Page design by   Susan Harring
Acquired for Parkhurst Brothers Publishers by   Ted Parkhurst

I dedicate this book to my grandfather,

Louis Eustice Herwig

a Twain-like character who gave me my sense of humor

and most likely saved my life.

ACKNOWLEDGMENTS

Recently, I have been fond of calling myself a Ray Bradbury Martian, meaning someone who becomes who they are by absorbing the culture and attitudes of those around them. Given people, opportunity and time, you can become anything. I became a storyteller, for instance, at the encouragement of my wife, but also because friends like Bob Pierce, Nadine Anderson, Dick Dice, Richard Sherburne and others came out to see my performances. Continued encouragement came from fellow members of the Ann Arbor Storytellers Guild, and from storytellers I have met at various conventions and events. Considering how many of them there are, it's impossible to call out all of them, and difficult to come up with a complete list.

That being said, I'd like to especially thank Beverly Black, Yvonne Healey, Judy Sima, Jeff Doyle, and Judy Schmidt for helping me in one way or another to move along the path that led to this book. I also want to call out Laura Lee Hayes for encouraging me to attend storytelling conferences and inviting me to co-host the monthly storytelling events that helped me move beyond telling and into a more active role. And thanks also to Jane Fink, who has supported me in many ways, who started me thinking about ways to modify Mark Twain's stories for a modern audience, and also for her comments on the manuscript. And thanks to Ted Parkhurst for understanding my ideas, for seeing the book in them, and for bringing it to life. Ok, I already mentioned my wife, but I have to tell you, she has this amazing ability to roll with the twists and turns as I follow my Martian sensibilities wherever they lead. I'm so grateful that she continues to share this journey into the unknown.

Steve Daut
Ann Arbor, 2018

TABLE OF CONTENTS

INTRODUCTION

When Samuel Langhorne Clemens was 18, he left home to work as a printer, and then from age 22 to 26, he worked on the river, becoming a licensed pilot before he left that life. One of the things he liked to do was go out on the sounding boats to measure the water depth with a sounding pole. Many of the poles were 12 feet long, with marks indicating depth in fathoms, each fathom being six feet. Most of the riverboats could navigate in less than one fathom. Anything more than that meant the way was clear, so full speed ahead. At the full depth of the pole, two fathoms, the call from sounder to wheelhouse would be "mark, twain." Clemens first wrote under the pen name of Mark Twain in 1863.

Samuel Clemens was not the first to write under that pen name. In *Life on the Mississippi*, he wrote about an ancient Mississippi mariner, Captain Isaiah Sellers, who apparently took his first steamboat trip in 1811, and was venerated even among the elder pilots of the day. Although not a writer himself, Captain Sellers occasionally would write short articles about the river for the *New Orleans Picayune* and sign them "Mark Twain." Clemens borrowed heavily from one of these essays for his own first newspaper article, earning him the lifelong ire of Captain Sellers. According to Clemens, the Captain never wrote another paragraph and never again used the name "Mark Twain," and when Captain Sellers died, Clemens adopted the name for his own writing.

Twain was an incredibly prolific writer. Not only was he a humorist and storyteller, but he had highly tuned hypocrisy and irony detectors, and a biting and insightful way of recording his findings. His articles and letters were published in the *Hannibal Journal, The Enterprise, The Golden Era, The Californian,* the *Sacramento Union, Alta California, New York Herald, New York Tribune, Galaxy Magazine,* and many other publications. He lectured on an immense array of topics and published not only novels but various collections of works that ranged from short stories to novellas and travelogues.

At times, it's hard to distinguish between his stories and his essays or rants. Some of that is by design, but some of it is most likely because his mind was free-ranging. Some of his stories lack any discernible structure, and many of them mix actual events with pure tall-tale-telling. But each one shows clearly the Twain style, which is characterized by intensely held positions, punctuated by wry and often biting humor, with a deep devotion to irony. Yet he does it with a humane graciousness that we all need to take note of these days. He showed a proclivity toward laughing at himself nearly as hard as he laughed at others, and that, perhaps, is Twain's best gift to us.

Even today, 160 years after he penned his first story, we still hear about Mark Twain. Perhaps someone read the "Jumping Frog" story to you as a child, and that's the last you heard about him. There are books available but few verbal presentations of his work. One reason may be the issue of story structure.

Audiences today like a story that has a shape and structure to it, and often an original Twain tale is more of an anecdote or a series of funny events with no discernible protagonist and antagonist except for a hapless Twain (or a character who is telling him a story) beset by the vagaries of life. A second reason may be, ironically, also one of the reasons for his success, which is his ability to turn a phrase in a way that laughs at itself by bringing in the ironies of the day. This can lead to verbose and quirky prose that has a tendency to freeze itself in time. The challenge of telling Twain for today's audience is to find the universal in his prose while updating the language to a pace and phrasing that doesn't distract a modern audience from the storyline.

Most of the more contemporary Twain books that I have run across are for children, which is ironic since Twain did not typically write for children. Even Hal Holbrook, who has presented his adult-geared program *Mark Twain Tonight* over 2100 times beginning in 1966, retired just this past year. It's prime time to make sure Twain's rich legacy is carried into the future.

Many of the stories in the book are highly condensed from their original form. The language and sentence structure have been simplified, while I've attempted to retain the character and insightful turns of phrase that are characteristic Twain. I have also built some classic structure into many of the retellings in this book, locking a hero and villain in a struggle, however inane the struggle might be. There are introductions to each of the stories, and with some, I add ideas or tips that might be helpful to tellers or readers. In addition, where the humor is tied to Twain's reaction to events of the time, I have tried to add in the things that audiences of Twain's time would be aware of in order to make the humor work. In a few cases, I have presented some alternative ways of telling in order to facilitate your success as a storyteller or reader of these stories.

With a number of the stories (eg., *My Watch*, *The McWilliamses and the Burglar Alarm*), Twain breaks up the original story with little subplots and asides that he revisits over and over again. Not only does that make the story sound repetitive in the telling, but I find it very easy to lose my place if I'm telling a story with that sort of structure. So I have extensively rearranged those stories to overcome my crummy memory. If you are able to keep track of where you are with the more complicated original structure, let me know, and I will worship at your storytelling feet.

When I began to consider how to arrange the stories in this book, I didn't want to simply default to a chronological listing because Twain has so many distinct narrative styles. I wanted to sort them out a bit. Twain eschewed categories, as I mentioned earlier, so putting the stories into distinct boxes is a bit tricky. At any rate, I have sorted the stories into what I consider personal narratives, stories inspired by current events, fables, and tall tales. A few of the stories fall into more than one category, so I put them into the one that seems the most prominent. Within each category, they are listed chronologically. Perhaps a more scholarly type would find my distinctions completely wrong, but philosophically, I have always felt that not knowing what you're doing is never a reason to avoid doing it. Regarding any creative pursuit, a former boss and mentor once told me, "If you know exactly what you're doing, you're already too late."

I started on this book after telling Twain tales for a few years, and also creating and telling my own stories. At one point, I was working on a new personal story when a storytelling friend, Laura Lee Hayes, commented that it sounded like Twain was beginning to inhabit my psyche. She hastened to add, "That's a really good thing." For the fun of it, I have concluded this book with that story, which you have my permission to tell as long as you begin with something like, "This story was told to me by a wonderful storyteller by the name of Steve Daut." Feel free to change the word "wonderful" to "brilliant," "incredible," "insightful," "hilarious," or some other highly complementary modifiers. Or all of the above.

Some quick notes regarding Copyright and Bibliography: According to reputable sources, including the United States Copyright office, any stories published before 1923 are in the public domain, and therefore may be freely quoted or reproduced in its entirety, without permission or fees. In addition, derivative works may also be created from them. The stories in this book are derived from originals first published in 1907 or earlier and are considered derivative works, which results in a mix of copyrighted and public domain bits in each of the stories. Every attempt has been made to find the earliest publication possible although that might not be the version I used. In every case, the source was published well before 1923. Sources are listed in the bibliography, and first publication dates are included with the title of each story. The bibliography also lists a number of references that may be of interest, including some original articles that are available in PDF format online through the Library of Congress. I didn't use all of them, but hey, I did the work of finding them so I figured I'd pass them along if anyone is interested. I also have listed *The Purloining of Prince Oleomargarine*, a newly published, illustrated children's book based on an unfinished Twain story that was recently discovered. I didn't use it for anything, but it's a pretty cool book.

The stories in this book can be read, but they are also designed to be told. Some of the longer ones are more of a challenge to tell, so rather than rote memorization, I tend to get the sense of the language used and the flow of events, then add a bit of improvisation to keep things lively. Frankly, some of the longer ones are just easier to read or condense even further. You are invited to take what works, modify it to meet your own needs and present it in a way that makes sense to you. To the extent that you borrow directly from this work in your own storytelling, I'd appreciate a nod of recognition according to your own conscience. On the other hand, please don't copy or post any of this in electronic, written, or another permanent form without first asking for permission.

Most of all, enjoy the stories!

TIPS FOR TELLING TWAIN

Everyone knows Mark Twain, or at least they know who he was. Tom Sawyer and Huck Finn are standard fare in children's literature, and in movies both realistic and animated. Some readers may know of Mark Twain from Hal Holbrook's 1967 movie, *Mark Twain Tonight*, or from Holbrook's performance tour. It seems to me that this is a blessing and a trap. Mark Twain was brilliant at branding himself with his shock of crazy white hair, his massive horseshoe mustache, and his characteristic vested white suit. This, of course, is the image that Holbrook used so effectively for 50 years.

But there is another Mark Twain behind that image, a Mark Twain who wrote and spoke passionately about social issues and reacted to the headlines of the day. Not all of Twain's work is light and humorous, or even contains the characteristic folksy quality that modern audiences expect of him. He wrote many articles anonymously, often taking radical or unpopular positions on social norms of the times. So if you are going to tell Mark Twain stories, you have a decision to make. Do you take the re-enactor role ala Holbrook and become the classic Twain persona, or do you scratch a little deeper and seek out Samuel Clemens, the real person behind the Twain stories?

I have chosen in this book, and also when I tell Twain stories, to honor the beauty and depth of each story by telling each in a way that grows out of my own personal style. Not only is a modern audience unlikely to sit through the original fifteen-thousand word original version of *Excerpt From Captain Stormfield's Visit to Heaven*, but lacking the historical context of much of the language, even if it is delivered flawlessly, not many people would understand more than half of it.

So the idea for me is to find the beauty, the irony, sarcasm, and sentimentality that Twain intended and discover my own way to deliver it to today's audiences. The thing that works best for me is to tip my hat to Twain (metaphorically or actually), and then tell each story in the way it demands. I tend to tell some stories like *A Medieval Romance* in a fairy-tale style, and *A Ghost Story* as if it is a Victorian Tale, because these seem to be the styles that Clemens was attempting to mimic. On the other hand, it feels more natural to adopt a folksy Twain-like style when telling *The Notorious Jumping Frog of Calaveras County*. But even when I tell Frog, the folksy style I adopt is one that flows naturally for me, not an imitation of what I imagine it would sound like from Twain's mouth. The idea is that I am serving the story, not my impression, or the audience's impression, of how Mark Twain would do it.

When it comes to telling these stories, I have found that less is more. Rather than a full-blown costume, I may don some clothes that invoke the 1860s – railroad pants and suspenders. When I tell *My Watch*, I might pull out a replica pocket watch, because younger audiences especially might not have any idea of what an actual watch looks like, and it's a stretch to expect them to understand a watch that doesn't run on a battery. A simple prop that you can pull out and demonstrate goes a long ways toward making the story come alive without a lot of explanation.

So to underscore the main thought here, I'd suggest that the best result comes from forgetting for a moment that the story was written by Mark Twain, and deciding the most effective way to bring your own style to the story. If you find a story of interest but have a hard time with the way it appears in this book, I've provided quite a bit of source material in the bibliography so that you can go back to the original and create a version that works better for you. Once you have found something that works for you, you might want to add a little introduction to put it into context. Feel free to use the introductory notes that I provide for the stories, or to delve into the fascinating history of each story on your own.

INTRODUCTION TO

CURING A COLD

I found this story in the May 24, 1867 issue of the *Marshall County Republican* (Plymouth, Indiana). As with many of Twain's articles, the original claims to be advice for readers and then progresses into a tall tale, with various asides to the readers to ground it as a true, but cautionary, tale. Because of Twain's original introduction, I included it here, rather in the section on tall tales. I also removed the asides, as they chopped up the narrative without much benefit, although I left the ending largely as it was. Twain's original introduction is as follows:

> It is a good thing, perhaps, to write for the amusement of the public, but it is a far higher and nobler thing to write for their instruction, their profit, their actual and tangible benefit. The latter is the sole object of this article. If it proves the means of restoring to health one solitary sufferer among my race, of lighting up once more the fire of hope and joy in his faded eyes, of bringing back to his dead heart again the quick, generous impulses of other days, I shall be amply rewarded for my labor; my soul will be permeated with the sacred delight a Christian feels when he has done a good, unselfish deed.

Having led a pure and blameless life, I am justified in believing that no man who knows me will reject the suggestions I am about to make, out of fear that I am trying to deceive him. Let the public do itself the honor to read my experience in doctoring a cold, as herein set forth, and then follow in my footsteps.

CURING A COLD

Adapted by Steve Daut,
Twain original first published in 1867

My constitution succumbed to a severe cold caused by undue exertion in getting ready to do something. The first time I began to sneeze, a friend told me to go and bathe my feet in hot water and go to bed. I did so. Shortly afterward, another friend advised me to get up and take a cold shower. I did that also. Within the hour another friend assured me that it was policy to "feed a cold and starve a fever." I had both. So I thought it best to fill myself up for the cold, and then stop eating and let the fever starve awhile.

In a case of this kind, I seldom do things by halves. I ate pretty heartily. I started down toward the office, and on the way encountered another bosom friend, who told me that a quart of salt water, taken warm, would come as near to curing a cold as anything in the world. I hardly thought I had room for it, but I tried it anyhow. The result was surprising. I believe I threw up my immortal soul.

It may be a good enough remedy, but I think it's too severe. If I had another cold in the head, and there were no course left me but to take either an earthquake or a quart of warm salt water, I would take my chances on the earthquake.

After the storm which had been raging in my stomach had subsided, and no more good Samaritans came along, I went on borrowing handkerchiefs again and blowing them to atoms, as had been my custom in the early stages of my cold. Then I came across a lady who had just arrived from over the plains and had from necessity acquired considerable skill in the treatment of simple "family complaints." I knew she must have a lot of experience, for she appeared to be a hundred and fifty years old.

She mixed a concoction composed of molasses, aqua fortis, turpentine and various other drugs, and instructed me to take a wine-glass full of it every fifteen minutes. I took one dose. That was enough. It robbed me of all moral principle, and awoke every unworthy impulse of my nature. Under its malign influence, my brain conceived miracles of meanness, but my hands were too feeble to execute them. If my strength had not surrendered to the succession of assaults from infallible cold remedies, I am convinced that I would have tried to rob the Graveyard.

Like most people, I often feel mean and act accordingly. But until I took that medicine, I had never reveled in such supernatural depravity and felt proud of it. At the end of two days, I was ready to go to doctoring again. I took a few more unfailing remedies and finally drove my cold from my head to my lungs.

I started coughing incessantly, and my voice fell to a thundering bass, two octaves below my natural tone. I could only fall to sleep by coughing myself into a state of utter exhaustion, and then the moment I began to talk in my sleep, my discordant voice woke me up again.

My case grew more and more serious every day. Plain gin was recommended. I took it. Then gin and molasses, and I took that also. Then gin and onions. I added the onions, and took all three. I detected no particular result, except that I had acquired breath like a buzzard's.

I decided to travel for my health. I went to Lake Bigler with my comrade, Wilson. We traveled in considerable style. We sailed and hunted and fished and danced all day, and I doctored my cough all night. I thought that all of this outdoor activity would help me to improve day by day. But my disease continued to grow worse.

A sheet bath was recommended. I had no idea what a sheet bath was, but had never rejected a remedy yet, so it seemed poor policy to refuse. It was administered at midnight, and the weather was very frosty. My breast and back were bared, and sheets soaked in ice water were wound round me until I resembled a swab for a muzzle-loading cannon.

It is a cruel expedient. When the chilly rag touched my warm flesh, it made me start with sudden violence and gasp for breath. It froze the marrow in my bones and stopped the beating of my heart. I thought my time had come.

When the sheet bath failed to cure my cough, a lady friend recommended the application of a mustard plaster to my breast. I believe that would have cured me effectually if it had not been for young Wilson. When I went to bed, I put my mustard plaster where I could reach it when I was ready for it. But young Wilson got hungry in the night and ate it.

Alter sojourning a week at Lake Bigler, I went to Steamboat Springs, and beside the steam baths, I took a lot of the vilest medicines that were ever concocted. They would have cured me, but I managed to aggravate my disease by carelessness and undue exposure.

Finally, a lady I met in San Francisco told me to drink a quart of whiskey every twenty-four hours, and another friend recommended precisely the same course. Each advised me to take a quart - that made half a gallon. I did it and still live.

Now, with the kindest motives in the world, I suggest that consumptive patients should try the variegated course of treatment I have gone through. If it doesn't cure them, it can't do more than kill them.

INTRODUCTION TO

THE KILLING OF JULIUS CAESAR

This story was first published in the compilation *The Celebrated Jumping Frog of Calaveras County, and Other Sketches.* It's a great little exercise in imagining what it was like to be a Roman Citizen, reading the newspaper accounts of the unfolding events. I have changed the name of the newspaper from the *Daily Evening Fasces*, to *The Daily Chariot*, Special Evening Edition because I didn't know the word Fasces, and that is the kind of little detail that can throw people out of the story.

I have simplified some of the names and tried to minimize the number of names, in order to make the action easier to follow. I have also converted the newspaper article to a more modern journalistic style, although I could only go so far lest it become over-sanitized and lose the voice of Mark Twain altogether. I've cut the newspaper account nearly in half as it is, but no doubt today it would be cut in half again and wedged between an advertisement for hair color and men's underwear.

In terms of story flow and progression, it is unchanged from the original.

THE KILLING OF JULIUS CAESAR "LOCALIZED"

Adapted by Steve Daut,
Twain original first published in 1867

Nothing in the world is so satisfying to a newspaper reporter as gathering up the details of a bloody and mysterious murder and writing them up with an emphasis on the mystery. It's the slant of the story that sets the reporter apart from those who have to work with the same facts. I have often felt regret that I was not reporting in Rome when Caesar was killed, especially for a newspaper that was willing to run a special evening edition in order to get at least twelve hours ahead of the morning-paper boys with this most magnificent scoop in history. Other events as startling as this have happened, but none that met all the characteristics of stories we so love today, magnified into sublime grandeur by the high rank, fame, and social and political standing of the actors in it. However, since I was not alive to report Caesar's assassination in the regular way, I can at least imagine it, as follows.

From *The Daily Chariot*, March 15, 44BC, Special Evening Edition:

Our usually quiet city of Rome was thrown into a state of

wild excitement yesterday by a bloody scene that sickens the heart and fills the soul with fear. All thinking men must ask, "What can be the future of our city where human life is held so cheaply and laws are so openly broken?"

It is our painful duty as journalists, to record the death of one of our most esteemed citizens, a man whose name is known throughout the empire, partly due to the efforts of *The Daily Chariot*. We refer to Mr. J. Caesar, the Emperor-elect.

This was an election battle, only one of a string of ghastly butcheries that have grown out of the jealousies and animosities engendered by these accursed elections. Rome would be better off if her very constables were elected to serve a century, for we have never been able to choose even a dog-catcher without a dozen knockdown fights, and without cramming the station-house with drunken vagabonds overnight.

It's said that when Caesar won the immense majority at the polls and the crown was offered to him, even his amazing unselfishness in refusing it three times was not sufficient to save him from whispered insults. These insults, of course, came from such men as Casca of the Tenth Ward, and other hirelings of the disappointed candidate, hailing mostly from the Eleventh and Thirteenth Wards.

We are further informed that many think the assassination of Julius Caesar was a put-up thing, a cut-and-dried arrangement hatched by Marcus Brutus and a lot of his hired roughs and carried out only too faithfully. Whether there are grounds for this suspicion or not, we leave to the people to judge for themselves, only asking that they read the following account carefully and dispassionately before they render their judgment.

The Senate was already in session. Caesar was coming down the street toward the capitol, conversing with some personal friends, and followed as usual by a large number of citizens. Just as he was passing in front of the D&T drug store, he observed casually that the Ides of March were come.

The reply was, "Yes, they are come, but not gone yet."

At this moment Artemus stepped up and asked Caesar to read a tract or something of the kind. Some later claimed that this was a note warning Caesar of the impending plot.

One of the Brutus gang stepped in and asked Caesar to instead read a missive of his own.

Artemus begged that Caesar read his immediately, because it was of personal consequence to Caesar. The thug of Brutus insisted that his was the most critical. Caesar shook them both off, and refused to read any petition in the street. He then entered the capitol, and the crowd followed him.

About this time a conversation was overheard that bears an appalling significance, considering the events.

Papilius "Pappy" Lena remarked to George Cassius that he hoped his enterprise to-day might thrive. When Cassius asked, "What enterprise?" Pappy only winked and said with simulated indifference, "Fare you well," then he sauntered toward Caesar.

Marcus Brutus himself asked what it was that Pappy had said. Allegedly, Cassius told him, and added in a low tone, "I fear our purpose is discovered." Whatever the exact exchange was, it led to a hushed conversation between Brutus, Cassius, and Casca. Investigators are still trying to discover the details of this conversation.

During this exchange, Caesar was talking to some of the back-country members about the approaching fall elections, and paying little attention to what was going on around him. He did not notice as Caesar's friend Mark Antony was drawn away, or as Brutus, with his gang of infamous desperadoes, closed around the doomed Caesar. One of the band knelt down and begged that the notorious criminal, Publius, might be recalled from banishment, but Caesar refused to grant his petition. A war of words began, and Casca instantly seized upon this shallow pretext for a fight. Casca sprang at Caesar and struck him with a small knife, then the others rushed upon him with their daggers drawn, but Caesar backed up to a statue of Pompey and was able to subdue them all with many blows of his powerful fists.

By this time the Senate was in an indescribable uproar. The throng of citizens in the lobbies had blocked the doors in their frantic efforts to escape from the building, the sergeant-at-arms and his assistants were struggling with the assassins. Venerable senators cast aside their encumbering robes and were leaping over benches and flying down the aisles in wild confusion toward the shelter of the committee-rooms, and a thousand voices were shouting "Police! Police"

Amid it all, great Caesar stood with his back against the statue, like a lion at bay, and fought his assailants weaponless, with the defiant bearing and unwavering courage which he had shown before on many a bloody field. But at last, when Caesar saw his old friend Brutus step forward armed with a murderous knife, it is said he seemed overpowered with grief and amazement, and dropped left his arm by his side. Hiding his face in the folds of his robe, he received the treacherous blow without any effort to stay the hand that gave it. He only said, *"Et tu, Brute?"* and fell lifeless on the marble pavement.

We learn that the robe Caesar had on when he was killed was found to be cut and gashed in no less than seven different places. There was nothing in the pockets. It will be exhibited at the coroner's inquest and will be damning proof of the killing.

LATER: While the coroner was summoning a jury, Mark Antony and other friends of the late Caesar got hold of the body, lugged it off to the Forum, and at last accounts Antony and Brutus were making speeches over it. They raised such a row among the people that, as we go to press, the chief of police believes there is going to be a riot, and is taking measures accordingly.

INTRODUCTION TO

JOURNALISM IN TENNESSEE

Research for this story really pushed my nerd buttons. Some sources said this story was written in 1871 and others said it was first published in 1869, two years before it was written. Subsequent discoveries by Albert Einstein about the nature of time notwithstanding, I realized there might be an issue in publishing an article before it was written. After some research, I was finally able to find a source that pinned down the first publication as the September 4, 1869 issue of the *Buffalo Express*.

Twain begins by implying that the inspiration for his story was the following comment by the editor of the *Memphis Avalanche* in answer to a correspondent who posted him as a Radical:— "*While he was writing the first word, the middle, dotting his i's, crossing his t's, and punching his period, he knew he was concocting a sentence that was saturated with infamy and reeking with falsehood.*"

Although I could not find the editorial he was referencing, I did find a fascinating exchange that occurred 30 years after *Journalism in Tennessee* was first published. It appears to be an actual exchange in the March 7, 1898 issue of *The Comet*

(Johnson City, Tennessee). I present a somewhat modernized interpretation of that exchange between three editors below. While it was clearly good-natured ribbing, it points out that journalistic warfare is a time-honored tradition.

"If editor Reaves of the *Hardeman Free Press* will visit Johnson City now, we will prepare a place for him in our new pest house and see that he is given three square meals a day and his regular medications."
– *The Comet*, Johnson City, Tennessee

"We very much deprecate *The Comet's* frivolous and ribald treatment of editor Reaves. Both *The Comet* and the Camden *Shillelah* are carrying their jealousy of the *Hardeman Free Press* too far. First, the *Shillelah* alludes to the editor of the *Free Press* as a microbe-smitten wart and the *Free Press* responds by denouncing the editor of the *Shillelah* as a red-nosed cherrybum. When *The Comet* then waltzes into the game and offers editor Reaves the freedom of their pest house, it does seem that a double-breasted gloom has settled over the journalism of Tennessee. Reaves is very much used to the luxury of his Bolivar lunatic asylum, so neither three square meals nor the medications *The Comet* offers him can make up for the insult they have dealt him. Unless *The Comet* can offer him an abundance of moonshine and designer cocktails, editor Reaves will prefer to stay at home, nurse his corns and let his intellect convalesce. We trust this journalistic warfare will now cease."
– *Memphis Commercial Appeal*

"If we were to accept the proposition from the Johnson City *Comet*, it might be a benefit to editor Lyle of *The Comet*. His medications would be reduced and his nose would be in a position to absorb enough sense from us to run a first-class weekly."

– *Hardeman Free Press*

Note to Storytellers:

The scenes of carnage in the following story are done in a slapstick way, and although they are the vehicle for the message, they are not the message itself. It is incredibly sad to me that I have to add this cautionary note, but consider the audience and the timing so that the humor does not get lost behind the imagery. While at first, the editorial feud in Twain's story seems over the top, there is a serious message in this story, which comes into stark relief today as the integrity of the press continues to be under fire. Somehow, knowing that "fake news" is an age-old question gives me an odd sense of relief.

JOURNALISM IN TENNESSEE

Adapted by Steve Daut,
Twain original first published in 1869

I was told by my doctor that a Southern climate would improve my health, so I went down to Tennessee and took a job with the *Morning Glory and Johnson County War-Whoop* as associate editor. When I went in the first day, I found the chief editor sitting tilted back in a three-legged chair with his feet on a pine table. There was another table and chair, and both were half buried under newspapers and scraps of manuscript. There was a wooden sandbox sprinkled with cigar stubs, and a stove with a door hanging by its upper hinge. The chief editor was wearing a long-tailed black frock-coat, a ruffled shirt, and white linen pants. His boots were small and neatly blacked. He was smoking a cigar and pawing his hair as he tried to think of a word.

I assumed that he was concocting a particularly knotty editorial. He told me to take the news exchanges, skim through them and write an article about the "Spirit of the Tennessee Press." I wrote as follows:

In their article about the Dallyhack railroad, the editors of the *Semi-Weekly Earthquake* have inadvertently left the town of Buzzardville off to one side. The gentlemen of the *Earthquake* will, of course, take pleasure in making the correction. We also observe that the editor of the *Mud Springs Morning Howl* has fallen into the error of supposing that Van Werter has not yet clinched the election, but no doubt the editor was simply misled by incomplete election returns. We also note that the city of Blathersville is contracting with some New York gentlemen to pave its well-nigh impassable streets with the Nicholson pavement. *The Daily Hurrah!* urges the measure, and seems confident of ultimate success.

I passed the manuscript over to the chief editor for acceptance, alteration, or destruction. He glanced at it and his face clouded. As he ran his eye down the pages, it was easy to see that something was wrong.

He sprang up and said, "Thunder and lightning! Do you suppose my subscribers are going to stand such gruel as that? Give me that pen!" I never saw a pen scrape and scratch its way so viciously, or plow through another man's verbs and adjectives so relentlessly.

While he was in the midst of his work, someone shot at him through the open window.

"Ah," said he, "that's that scoundrel Smith, of the *Moral Volcano*. He was due yesterday." He snatched a navy revolver from his belt and fired. Smith dropped, shot in the thigh. As he dropped, his gun went off, but he only shot off one of my fingers. Then a hand grenade came down the stove-pipe, and the explosion shivered the stove into a thousand fragments. However, it did no further damage, except that a vagrant piece of the stove knocked a couple of my teeth out.

"That stove is utterly ruined," said the chief editor. "Well, no matter. Now, here is the way this stuff ought to be written."

The manuscript was scarred with erasures and line-outs till its mother wouldn't know it. It now read as follows:

> The inveterate liars of the *Semi-Weekly Earthquake* are evidently trying to palm off on the public another vile and brutal falsehood with regard to the Ballyhack railroad. They had better swallow the lie that Buzzardville should be left off at one side if they want to save their abandoned reptile carcasses from the cowhiding they so richly deserve. We observe that the blackhearted scoundrel of the *Mud Springs Morning Howl* is once again degrading his office by spreading the falsehood that Van Werter is not elected. Blathersville wants a Nicholson pavement, but the idea of a pavement in a one-horse town composed of two gin-mills and a blacksmith shop is insane. Yet that mustard-plaster of a newspaper, *The Daily Hurrah!*, is braying about what a good idea it is.

"Now that's the way to write— peppery and to the point instead of that mush-and-milk journalism you wrote."

About this time a brick came through the window with a splintering crash and gave me a considerable jolt in the back. I began to feel in the way, so I move out of range. Then a large man in military regalia appeared in the door a moment afterward with a dragoon revolver in his hand.

He said, "Sir, have I the honor of addressing the poltroon who edits this mangy sheet?"

"You have," said my editor. "I believe I have the honor of addressing the putrid liar, Colonel Blatherskite Tecumseh?"

"Right, Sir. I have a little account to settle with you. If you're at leisure, we will begin."

"Well, I'm trying to finish an article on 'Encouraging Progress of Moral and Intellectual Development in America', but there is no hurry. Begin."

Both pistols rang out their fierce clamor at the same instant. The chief lost a lock of his hair, and the Colonel's bullet ended its career in the fleshy part of my thigh. The Colonel's left shoulder was clipped a little. They fired again. Both missed their men this time, but I got my share, a shot in the arm. At the third fire, both gentlemen were wounded slightly, and I had a knuckle chipped. I then said I believed I would go out and take a walk, as this was a private matter. But both gentlemen begged me to keep my seat, and assured me I was not in the way. The sixth shot mortally wounded the Colonel, who remarked, with fine humor, that he would have to take his leave, as he had business uptown. He inquired the way to the undertaker's, and then he left.

The chief turned to me and said, "I'm expecting company for dinner, and need to get ready. It will be a favor to me if you read these proofs and attend to the customers. Jones will be here at three. Whip him with one of the cowhides under the table. Gillespie will call earlier. Throw him out the window. Ferguson will be along about four. Kill him with one of the weapons in the drawer there. That's all for today, I believe. In case of an accident, go to Lancet, the surgeon, downstairs. We trade his services for advertising." Then he was gone.

The perils I went through over the next three hours were so awful that I lost all peace of mind and cheerfulness. Gillespie had thrown me out of the window, Jones bested me in the cowhiding, I had lost my scalp in an encounter with a stranger, and I was left a wreck and ruin of chaotic rags. And at last, at bay in the corner, and beset by an infuriated mob of editors, blacklegs, politicians, and desperadoes, who raved and swore and flourished their weapons, I was in the act of resigning my position on the paper when the chief arrived with a rabble of friends. Then ensued a scene of riot and carnage such as no human pen can describe. People were shot, probed, dismembered, blown up, thrown out of the window. After this tornado of activity, it was all over. In five minutes there was silence, and the gory chief and I sat alone and surveyed the ruin-strewn floor.

He said, "You'll like this place when you get used to it."

I said, "You need to excuse me, perhaps I could write to suit you after a while, but to speak the plain truth, I can't write with comfort when I am interrupted as much as I have been today. I never before had such a spirited time in all my life, and I like your calm unruffled way of explaining things to the customers, but you see I am not used to it. Southern hospitality does not suit me, and I fear the paragraphs which I have written today will wake up another nest of hornets. The mob of editors will come again and will want somebody for breakfast. But I came South for my health, and I will go back on the same errand. Tennessee journalism is too stirring for me."

We parted with mutual regret, and I retired to the hospital.

INTRODUCTION TO

MY WATCH

This story is, frankly, a bit of a challenge for a modern audience. The technology has changed so much that you have to know your audience to tell the story so that everyone understands the humor. I have modified the beginning to try and bridge that gap for a modern audience. But increasingly with younger people, you may even have to explain what a watch is. Still, I wanted to include the story because it shows the depth of Twain's inventiveness in his ability to take a simple idea and thoroughly exploit a wide range of comedic possibilities through the various ways that a piece of technology can go haywire, especially when aided and abetted by a bunch of incompetent, or possibly unscrupulous, repairmen.

MY WATCH

Adapted by Steve Daut,
Twain original first published in 1870

Back in the day, every watch used to stand on its own time. There weren't any satellites to beam the time down at you from the universe, so the poor watches had to figure out for themselves what time it was and if they got it wrong, well, they might not even know it until their owner, or the watchmaker, set them straight. It could take months before a watch got back on track with the rest of the world. And there weren't any diamonds or batteries in them. You had to wind them up, and they were full of springs and wheels and all such-like that. They would wind down, and then you'd have to wind them up again, two or three times every day. And watches knew their place. You had a special pocket in your pants or your vest where the watch lived. You didn't wear them on your wrist or around your neck, and a watch would never hide inside a telephone. If you had a watch that kept good time, it was a thing of beauty.

Well, I had a watch like that. It ran perfectly for eighteen months. It didn't break down or stop or anything like that and it didn't gain or lose even a minute. Well, one night, I let it run down. This was sort of an omen, a forerunner of calamity.

I wound it up and set it best as I could figure and took it to the jeweler to set the exact time. He asked if I had ever had it repaired and I told him it didn't need to be repaired, just set to the right time. He pried it open, did a little test and declared it was running slow and needed the regulator sped up. I tried to tell him I was the regulator and I'd fallen down on the job, but this human cabbage wouldn't listen.

He set the regulator up, and that watch began to gain. It went faster and faster every day. Within the week its pulse went up to 150 in the shade, and within months it was thirteen days ahead of time. Come Halloween that watch was already in the first snow of December. It got to the place that it was making me pay my monthly house rent every two weeks.

I couldn't afford that, so I took it to another feller. He said on top of regulating, it needed cleaning and oiling. So he did all that, and the thing slowed down to where everything went by like one of them slow-motion movies. I started missing appointments, then my dinner, then days at a time. A couple of weeks down the road it was a day behind. In another two weeks, I was living in the day before yesterday. It got so bad that I'd go down to the museum and get my current news from the mummy.

I went to another watchmaker and he said the case was warped so he'd have to ream it out. Well, after that, the thing averaged the right time but nothing more. For a half day it would go like the Devil on fire, then it would slow down to the speed of frozen molasses. By the end of the day, it would be right on time again. So at the end of the day, it did its job, but in the in-between, it wasn't worth much.

The next feller told me the king-bolt was broken. I had no idea what a king-bolt was, but I didn't want to sound ignorant so I had him fix that. Well, after that it would run awhile and stop awhile, using its own discretion about the intervals. I never knew when it was going to be running and when it was going to be stopped, so I took it to another fella who told me there was something wrong with the hair trigger. After he fixed that, it would run fine until ten minutes to ten, when both of the arms would stick together like a pair of scissors and it was impossible to tell what time it was.

Well, one feller unbent the crystal and another one rewound the mainspring and yet another one said half the works needed re-soling, whatever that was. Finally, they got the thing to working all right except every eight hours it would take to buzzing like a bee and the hands would stand straight up and start spinning around like a flywheel, then stop with a bang. Then it would start up again and be OK for another eight hours. And every time it went off it kicked back like a musket. After a while, I was getting pretty sore around my watch pocket so I tried one more time.

Finally, I took it to a feller who took the whole thing apart right in front of my eyes, and I realized this thing was getting serious. The watch had cost me two hundred dollars to begin with and so far the repairs had come to around three thousand, so I kept a close eye on this guy. Then I recognized this watchmaker as an old steamboat engineer I used to know, and not a very good engineer, either.

As he was poking through all those wheels and springs he said, "This watch makes too much steam. You need to hang a monkey wrench on the safety valve."

Well, I have to admit I was a little perturbed with this fella and I brained him on the spot. It was actually pretty satisfying too, and I was happy to pay for the hospital bill out of my own pocket.

My Uncle Will used to say that a good horse is a good horse until it had run away once, and a good watch was a good watch until the repairers get a chance at it. Guess I should have listened to him and tossed that thing away after the first time it went wrong.

INTRODUCTION TO

POLITICAL ECONOMY

In this story, Twain does a bit of a bait and switch. You think you are going to hear a story about, well, political economy, but it's actually about a number of things, primarily the dumb decisions we make when we are trying to stay focused on something but we keep getting distracted. But, in a topic that shows up often with Twain, it is also about the dumb decisions we make because we don't want to admit our ignorance, and the dumb decisions we make when we let a smooth-talking salesman dominate us. Are you beginning to sense a theme here?

At any rate, the original story elaborates on the essay that Twain is trying to write in the story. He picks up and drops elaborate and esoteric arguments regarding political economy in mid-sentence, perhaps with the intent of having us experience the same frustration that he is experiencing at the constant interruptions. The problem with this is that if you try to focus on the words of the essay the narrator is trying to write, it chops up the action of the actual story. This technique is difficult in the telling and also distracting for an audience. So in this version, after the first couple of times he goes back to the words of the essay, I instead describe his vain attempts to refocus on the essay he is trying to write, without providing the confusing details of the essay itself.

Twain also invokes an invisible intermediary to answer the door for him, which is the kind of thing that some audience members find so distracting that it throws them out of the story because they spend their time wondering who that invisible person is. I eliminated the middle-person and have Twain answer his own door.

POLITICAL ECONOMY

Adapted by Steve Daut,
Twain original first published in 1870

I had just settled in to complete the essay that was due to go to press the next morning. It was not going well. So far, it had taken me two hours to write the following:

Political Economy is the basis of all good government. The wisest men of all ages have brought to bear upon this subject the

… Then I was interrupted by the doorbell. I went down to find a stranger at the door. I confronted him and asked to know his business, struggling all the time to keep a tight rein on my seething political-economy ideas, and not let them break away from me.

Privately, I wished the stranger was in the bottom of the canal with a cargo of wheat on top of him. I was all in a fever from my writing, but he was cool. He said he was sorry to disturb me, but as he was passing he noticed that I needed some lightning-rods. I said, "Yes, yes, go on. What about it?" He said there was nothing about it in particular, except that he would like to put them up for me.

I'm new to housekeeping since I have lived in hotels and boarding-houses most of my life. But like anybody else of similar experience, I try to appear to strangers to be more experienced than I am, so I said in an offhand way that I had been intending for some time to have six or eight lightning-rods put up.

The stranger gave me a strange look, but complimented me on my thoroughness and said he'd get started right away. I said, "All right," and started off to wrestle with my great subject again, when he called me back and said it would be necessary to know exactly how many "points" I wanted to be put up, what parts of the house I wanted them on, and what quality of rod I preferred.

Though I was, at this point, thoroughly distracted, I tried to get through the discussion, hoping he would not suspect that I was a novice. I told him to put up eight "points," put them all on the roof, and use the best quality of rod. He said he could furnish the plain article at 20 cents a foot, copper at 25 cents, or zinc-plated spiral-twist at 30 cents. He said the zinc would stop a streak of lightning any time, no matter where it was bound, and render its errand harmless and its further progress apocryphal.

I said apocryphal was no slouch of a word, so I liked the spiral-twist and would take that brand. Then he went on some long-winded discussion about how many feet of wire it would take to do the job, once again lunging into the type of wire involved and the difference between economy and the best possible job of it, and I told him to make any kind of a job he pleased out of it, but to just let me get back to my work.

So I got rid of him at last and after half an hour spent in getting my train of political-economy thoughts coupled together again, I was ready to go on once more. I stared at the words I had written...

Political Economy is the basis of all good government. The wisest men of all ages have brought to bear upon this subject the

... And I began to ponder who the wisest men of all ages might be. Zoroaster, perhaps, or Horace Greeley?

Here I was interrupted again, and I went down to confer further with that lightning-rod man. My mind was hot and frenzied with thoughts of wise men throughout history as I confronted the man, who was calm and sweet, standing in the contemplative attitude of the Colossus of Rhodes, with one foot on my infant rose bush and the other among my pansies, gazing critically and admiringly in the direction of my main chimney. He said, "Have you ever seen anything more deliriously picturesque than eight lightning-rods on one chimney?"

Hoping that we were done with the project, I said I had no present recollection of anything that transcended it. But apparently, this didn't properly assuage his ego. He said, "All that's needed now to make your house a perfect balm to the eye, is to touch up the other chimneys a little, and thus add a soothing uniformity of achievement that would allay the excitement naturally consequent upon the *coup d'etat*." I complimented him on his verbosity, and he began to discuss the details of his plan.

I told him I was in a dreadful hurry, and I wished we could get this business permanently mapped out, so that I could go on with my work. At this point, he seemed terribly hurt, as if my deadline was somehow impugning his artistry.

He said, "I could have put up those eight rods, and marched off about my business. Some men would have done it. But no. I said to myself, 'This man is a stranger to me, and I will die before I'll wrong him.' But I see that I've imposed on your precious time, so I'll be on my way, and if the undisciplined and incandescent messenger of heaven strikes your house, then—"

"There, now, stop it. Go ahead and put on the other eight, add five hundred feet of spiral-twist. Do anything and everything you want to do, but calm your sufferings and try to keep your feelings where you can reach them with the dictionary. Meanwhile, if we understand each other now, I will go to work again."

I sat at my desk for a full hour after that, staring at my meager half-sentence, trying to get back to where I was when my train of thought was broken up by the last interruption. I was just on the verge of a linguistic breakthrough when the lightning-rod man rang again. I went down in a state of mind bordering on impatience.

He said he would rather have died than interrupt me, but he had rerun the calculations and saw that if a thunderstorm were to come up and the house stood there with nothing on earth to protect it but sixteen lightning-rods—"

"Let us have peace!" I shrieked. "Put up a hundred and fifty! Put some on the kitchen! Put a dozen on the barn! Put a couple on the cow! Put one on the cook! Scatter them all over the persecuted place till it looks like a zinc-plated, spiral-twisted, silver-mounted wheat field! Move! Use up all the material you can get your hands on, and when you run out of lightning-rods put up ramrods, cam-rods, stair-rods, piston-rods—anything that will pander to your dismal appetite for artificial scenery, and bring respite to my raging brain and healing to my lacerated soul!"

Wholly unmoved and smiling sweetly, this iron man said he would do as I asked.

I went back to my desk, wholly disgusted with the matter. Fortunately, my heated state lubricated my pen, and I wrote in a blind fury, though the essay diverted into poetry, science, and philosophy. There was not a word or phrase that had anything to do with political economy.

When the doorbell rang again, I rushed down to get it.

"Now, not a word out of you— not a single word. Just state your bill and relapse into impenetrable silence forever and ever on these premises. Nine hundred, dollars? Is that all?" I paid him gladly and sent him on his way.

As he left, I noticed the multitude of people gathering in the street to stare and point at my roof. Bless my life, had they never seen lightning-rods before? Three days later, the house was the talk and wonder of the town. The theaters languished, for their happiest scenic inventions were tame and commonplace compared with my lightning-rods. Our street was blocked night and day with spectators.

It was a blessed relief on the second day when a thunderstorm came up and the lightning began. It cleared the galleries. In five minutes there was not a spectator within half a mile of my place. And that was just as well, for all the falling stars and Fourth-of-July fireworks of a generation, put together and rained down simultaneously out of heaven in one brilliant shower upon one helpless roof, would not outshine or out flash the pyrotechnic display that was making my house so magnificently conspicuous in the general gloom of the storm. By actual count, the lightning struck at my establishment seven hundred and sixty-four times in forty minutes. Nothing was ever seen like it since the world began.

At last the awful siege came to an end, because there was absolutely no more electricity left in the clouds above us within grappling distance of my insatiable rods. Then I sallied forth, gathered fearless workmen together, and not a bite or a nap did we take till the premises were utterly stripped of all their terrific armament except just three rods on the house, one on the kitchen, and one on the barn. And after a time, people began to use our street again.

I will remark here, in passing, that during that fearful time I did not continue my essay upon political economy. I am not even yet settled enough in nerve and brain to resume it.

INTRODUCTION TO

HOW I EDITED AN AGRICULTURAL PAPER

This story is based on an article that appeared simultaneously in the July, 1870 *Galaxy Magazine* and the July 2, 1870 issue of the *Buffalo Express*, with slightly different titles. I also found a short version in the December 1, 1870 edition of the *Democratic Press*, entitled "Mark Twain as an Agricultural Editor." I don't know if he was actually asked to edit an agricultural paper in the regular editor's absence. Twain had a way of starting with reality and then taking it to ridiculous extremes in the best tradition of tall tale tellers.

If this is based on a real incident, my guess is he didn't last long because he did have a way of stretching the limits of editorial credulity during his days at the *Buffalo Express*. In fact, it is likely that the rant toward the end of this story is a fairly accurate depiction of arguments he had with his business partners George H. Selkirk and Josephus Nelson Larned, more traditional newspapermen who, though the circulation of the paper had increased significantly during Twain's tenure, were uncomfortable with his freewheeling style of writing and his blurring of the line between fact and fiction. Ultimately, Twain tired of the restrictive environment of journalism, so he sold out his share and left the paper in 1871.

HOW I EDITED AN AGRICULTURAL PAPER

Adapted by Steve Daut,
Twain original first published in 1870

I had misgivings about taking temporary editorship of an agricultural paper, the same way a landlubber might feel upon taking command of a ship. But salary was an object, given my circumstances, so I agreed to step in while the regular editor went off for holiday. It felt luxurious to be editing again and I threw myself into the work. We went to press that very day, and as I went home I noted various groups of people staring and pointing at me. The same curious crowd followed me as I went to work the next morning, and I reveled in my newfound celebrity.

I had been at it half an hour when an old gentleman with a flowing beard and austere face came up to me, paper in hand.

"Are you the new editor?"

"That would be me."

"Have you ever edited an agricultural paper before?"

"No," I said. "This is my first attempt."

"Very likely. Have you ever had any experience in agriculture, practically?"

"No, I believe I have not."

"Some instinct told me so," said the old gentleman, putting on his spectacles, looking over them at me with disgust. "Let me read you what gave me that instinct. It was this editorial. Listen, and see if it was you that wrote it:"

"Turnips should never be pulled—it injures them. It is much better to send a boy up and let him shake the tree."

"Now what do you think of that?" He continued, "I really suppose you wrote it."

"Think of it? Why, I think it is good. I think it is sense. I have no doubt that every year, millions and millions of bushels of turnips are spoiled in this township alone by being pulled in a half-ripe condition, when, if they had sent a boy up to shake the tree…"

"Shake your grandmother! Turnips don't grow on trees!"

"Oh, they don't, don't they? Well, who said they did? The language was intended to be figurative. Anybody that knows anything will know that meant that the boy should shake the vine."

Then this old person got up and tore his paper into shreds, stamped on them, broke several things with his cane and said I didn't know as much as a cow, and then went out. I fancied he was displeased about something, but not knowing what the trouble was, I couldn't be any help to him.

Not long afterward appeared a long cadaverous creature with shoulder-length locks and a week's stubble on his face. Highly agitated, he looked right and left to make certain no one but me was in the room, then he thrust a paper at me and demanded that I read from it.

"The guano is a fine bird, but it must be reared with care, imported only between June and September, and kept in a warm place during the winter months."

"The grain season appears to be moving backward, so buckwheat cakes should be planted in July instead of August."

"The pumpkin berry is a favorite with the natives of New England, preferring it to gooseberries when making fruitcake. It is the only member of the orange family that will thrive in the North, except the gourd and one or two varieties of squash. But planting it in the front yard with the shrubbery is fast going out of vogue because it has been found to be a failure as a shade tree."

Here he stopped my reading, sprang toward me, and shook my hand vigorously. "Thank you, thank you," said he. "I thought I had gone crazy, for after reading this I set fire to my house and have probably crippled half a dozen people in my frenzy to get here. But now you have confirmed that I actually read this insanity, I can rest easy, knowing that my mind has stood the strain of one of your articles" At this, he hopped off, overjoyed.

I felt a bit uncomfortable with the arsons and cripplings this wild man had entertained himself with, feeling remotely accessory to them. But my musings were quickly banished when the regular editor walked in, clearly having cut short his trip to Egypt.

He surveyed the damage done by the last two visitors, heaved a deep sigh, and said, "Well, the physical mess here is not the worst of it. I fear that the reputation of the paper is permanently injured. True, the paper has never sold such a large edition or soared to such celebrity, but we'd prefer not to be famous for lunacy, or prosper from infirmities of the mind. There are crowds gathered on the streets, all trying to get a glimpse of you, thinking you are insane. Whatever put it into your head that you could edit a paper of this nature? It couldn't be worse if I thought you had actually calculated to destroy this paper. You don't seem to have even the rudiments of agriculture. Why didn't you tell me that?"

I replied, "Tell you? What in the world should I need to tell you, you cabbage, you son of a cauliflower? I have been in the editorial business going on fourteen years and it's the first time I've ever heard that a man has to know anything in order to edit a newspaper. Who writes critiques of drama for second-rate newspapers? Shoemakers and apprentice pharmacists, that's who. Who writes book reviews? People who never wrote one. No political pundit has ever successfully run for office. Don't you try to tell me anything about the newspaper business, you turnip!"

"But since you chose to treat me as I have been treated, I'm happy to leave this place behind. I have done my duty and fulfilled my contract. I told you I could make this paper of interest to all classes, and so I have. If I had two more weeks, I could run your circulation up to twenty-thousand, well beyond the meager agricultural sorts that read it now. In fact, most likely there would be nary a farmer left by the time I was done. You are the loser in this rupture, not me, you potted plant. Adios!"

Then I left.

INTRODUCTION TO

ARGUING WITH A RAVEN

This story is a nearly word-for-word portion of the original version that was published in the *Cincinnati Daily Star* on May 18, 1880. The article that contained this story was published as an excerpt from Twain's *A Tramp Abroad* to promote the book.

ARGUING WITH A RAVEN

Adapted by Steve Daut,
Twain original first published in 1880

The world was bright with sunshine outside, but a deep and mellow twilight reigned in the deep woods, and also a silence so profound that I seemed to hear my own breathing. When I stood ten minutes, thinking and imagining, and getting my spirit in tune with the place, a raven suddenly uttered a hoarse croak over my head. It made me jump, and then I was angry because I jumped. I looked up, and the creature was sitting on a limb right over me, looking down at me. I felt something of the same sense of humiliation and injury that a person feels when he finds that a human stranger has been clandestinely inspecting him in his privacy, and mentally commenting upon him. I eyed the raven, and the raven eyed me. Nothing was said during some seconds. Then the bird stepped a little way along his limb to get a better point of observation, lifted his wings, stuck his head far down below his shoulders toward me, and croaked again. It was a croak with a distinctly insulting expression about it. If he'd spoken in English he could not have said any more plainly than he did say in Raven, "Well, what do you want here?"

I felt as foolish as if I had been reproved for some mean act. However, I made no reply. I would not bandy words with a raven. The adversary waited awhile with his shoulders still lifted, his head thrust down between them, and his keen bright eye fixed on me. Then he threw out two or three more insults that I could not understand. But I knew that at least some of the insults consisted of language not used in church.

I still made no reply. The adversary raised his head and called. There was an answering croak from a little distance in the wood, evidently a croak of inquiry. The adversary explained with enthusiasm, and the other raven dropped everything and came. The two sat side by side on the limb and discussed me as freely and offensively as two great naturalists might discuss a new kind of bug. The thing became more and more embarrassing. They called in another friend.

This was too much. I saw that they had the advantage of me, and so I decided to get out, just walk away. They enjoyed my defeat completely. They craned their necks and laughed at me. They squawked insulting remarks after me as long as they could see me.

They were nothing but ravens. I knew that what they thought about me was of no consequence and yet when even a raven shouts after you, "What a strange hat!" or "Oh, pull down your vest!" and that sort of thing, it hurts you and humiliates you, and there is no getting around it with fine reasoning and petty arguments.

INTRODUCTION TO

THE PROFESSOR'S YARN

This story is imbedded in Chapter 36 of *Life on the Mississippi*, and is a classic Twain tale about the rollicking world of riverboat gambling. The tale takes me back to my own youth, growing up on the Mississippi, riding on the Delta Queen, and watching endless episodes of Brett Maverick as he plied his trade with a wink and a grin.

THE PROFESSOR'S YARN

Adapted by Steve Daut,
Twain original first published in 1883

It was in the early days. I wasn't a college professor then, just a humble-minded young land-surveyor with the world to survey, in case anybody wanted it done. I had a contract to survey a route for a great mining ditch in California, and I was on my way by sea, a month-long journey around the Cape and up along the west coast of South America. I avoided conversation with the other passengers in favor of reading and dreaming. There were three professional gamblers on board. They were rough, repulsive fellows. I never talked with any of them, yet I couldn't avoid them. They gambled in an upper-deck stateroom every day and night, and I often caught glimpses of them through the door, which stood ajar to let out the surplus tobacco smoke and profanity. They were an evil and hateful presence.

There was one other passenger who seemed determined to be friendly with me, and I couldn't get rid of him without hurting his feelings. Besides, there was something engaging in his countrified simplicity and his beaming good nature. The first time I saw this Mr. John Backus, he had the manner of a rancher or farmer from the backwoods of some western State, and it turned out he was exactly that, a cattle rancher from Ohio. He got to dropping alongside me every day after breakfast, and we took long promenades around the decks of the ship. In the course of time, I got to know everything about his business, his prospects, his family, his relatives, his politics, and despite my general inclination to keep private, he managed to get out of me everything I knew about my trade, my tribe, my purposes, my prospects, and myself.

I said something about triangulation once, and he asked what it meant. I explained that it was a way of drawing a triangle on a map to locate yourself. After that, he quietly and inoffensively ignored my name, and always called me Triangle.

What an enthusiast he was in cattle! At the bare name of a bull or a cow, his eyes would light up and his eloquent tongue would turn itself loose. He knew all breeds, he loved all breeds, he caressed them all with his affectionate tongue. When I couldn't take the cattle talk anymore I would change the subject and he would listen politely, but all of the life would drain out of him on any topic but that of the bovine kind.

One day he said, a little hesitatingly, "Triangle, would you mind coming down to my stateroom a minute, and have a little talk on a certain matter?"

I went with him at once. As soon as we got there, he put his head out the door, glanced up and down the hall warily, then closed the door and locked it. He sat down on the sofa, and said, "I'm going to make you a little proposition, and if it strikes you favorable, it'll be a good thing for both of us. Mind you, I'm only letting you see this because we've gotten to know each other and I trust you like an old friend already. I've raked and scraped and saved a considerable many years, and everything I've got is all here."

He unlocked an old trunk, tumbled a chaos of shabby clothes aside, drew a short stout bag into view for a moment, then buried it again and relocked the trunk. Dropping his voice to a cautious low tone, he continued, 'She's all there—around ten thousand dollars. Being as I'm a cattleman and you're a surveyor, this is my idea. I know, and you know, that all along a line that's being surveyed, there's little triangles of land that get missed, and they fall to the surveyor free gratis for nothing. All you've got to do, on your side, is to survey in such a way that these free lands will fall on good fat land. I'll stock 'em with cattle, in rolls the cash, and I plunk out your share of the dollars on a regular basis."

I was sorry to wither his blooming enthusiasm, but it couldn't be helped. I interrupted, and said severely, "I'm not that kind of a surveyor. Let's change the subject, Mr. Backus."

It was pitiful to see his confusion and hear his awkward and shamefaced apologies. He didn't seem to have suspected that there was anything improper in his proposition, but when he saw my reaction, he appeared horrified. I hastened to console him and lead him on to forget his mishap in a conversation about cattle and butchering. As we went on deck, it happened luckily that we were in port at Acapulco and the crew was just beginning to hoist some cattle aboard in slings. Backus's melancholy vanished instantly, and with it the memory of his late mistake. "Now look at that! If the folks back in Ohio could see cattle being moved like that, their eyes would just bug out of their heads."

All the passengers were on deck to look, even the gamblers. Apparently, the gamblers had overheard us talking, and they moved in close to listen. Backus seemed to know them all and began to regale them with his pet topic. They were asking him all sort of questions about what kind of cows they were and how much they must weigh and all such like. As I moved away, I saw the conversation continued between the four men. Then it grew earnest and quiet. They started talking to him in hushed tones. Backus gradually pulled away but the gamblers followed. I was uncomfortable, but as they passed by me I heard Backus say, with a tone of persecuted annoyance, "It ain't any use, gentlemen. I warn't raised to gambling, and I ain't a-going to risk it."

I felt relieved, assuring myself that his level head would protect him from those predators. But during the fortnight's run from Acapulco to San Francisco I often saw the gamblers talking earnestly with Backus. Once I threw out a gentle warning to him, but he chuckled comfortably and said, "Yes, they tag around after me, wanting me to play a little, just for amusement, they say. But if my folks have told me once to look out for that sort of livestock, they've told me a thousand times, I reckon."

Soon we were approaching San Francisco. It was an ugly black night, with a strong wind blowing. I was on deck, alone. Toward ten I started below, and I saw Backus coming out from the gambler's den. I flew down the companion-way, looked around for him, could not find him, then returned to the deck just in time to catch a glimpse of him as he re-entered that confounded nest of rascality. Had he yielded at last? I feared it. Had he gone below for his bag of cash?

I drew near the door, full of foreboding. It was open a crack, and I glanced in and saw a sight that made me bitterly wish I had given my attention to saving my poor cattleman-friend, instead of reading and dreaming my foolish time away. He was gambling. Worse still, he was being plied with champagne and was already showing some effect from it. He praised the cider, as he called it, and said that it was so good he almost believed he would drink it even if it was spirits.

Surreptitious looks passed from one rascal to another, and they filled all the glasses, and while Backus honestly drained his to the bottom they pretended to do the same, but threw the wine over their shoulders. I couldn't bear to watch, so I wandered forward and tried to interest myself in the sea and the voices of the wind. But my uneasy spirit kept dragging me back at quarter-hour intervals. Through the night, I watched the same scene over and over again, Backus drinking his wine and the others throwing theirs away.

The only hope I had was that we would reach our anchorage quickly, and that would break up the game. I helped the ship along all I could with my prayers, and finally, we went booming through the Golden Gate.

Back at the gambler's den, there was small room for hope. Backus's eyes were heavy and bloodshot, his sweaty face was crimson, his speech maudlin and thick, his body sawed drunkenly about with the weaving motion of the ship. The cards were dealt and Backus took his hand, glanced at it, and his dull eyes lit up for a moment. The gamblers saw it and got ready to move in for the kill.

"How many cards?" the dealer asked.

"None," said Backus.

The villains each took a card or two and the betting began. So far, the bets had been a dollar or two, but Backus started off with a ten. Wiley hesitated a moment, then went ten dollars better. The other two threw up their hands. Backus went twenty better. Wiley said, "I see that, and raise you a hundred!" then smiled and reached for the money.

"Let it alone," said Backus, with drunken gravity.

"What? You mean to say you're going to cover it?"

"Cover it? Well, I reckon I am— and lay another hundred on top of it, too." He reached down inside his overcoat and produced the required sum.

This went on for a bit longer, Backus in a drunken frenzy to match everything that wolf came at him with, until ten thousand dollars was laid out on the table. Backus reached into his coat and tossed his golden shot-bag on the pile. Wiley called and the bet was made for every dime Backus had.

"What have you got?" asked Backus.

"Four kings, you durn fool!" Wiley threw down his cards and surrounded the stakes with his arms.

"Four aces!" thundered Backus, covering his man with a cocked revolver.

"I'm a professional gambler myself, and I've been laying for you duffers for this whole voyage!"

Down went the anchor, and the long trip was ended.

Well, it's a sad world. One of the three gamblers was Backus's pal. It was he that dealt the fateful hands. According to an understanding with the two victims, he was supposed to give Backus four queens, but of course, he had made other arrangement with Backus.

A week later, I stumbled upon Backus, dressed to the teeth, in Montgomery Street.

As we were parting, he said, cheerily, "By the way, you needn't mind about that little surveying proposal. I don't really know anything about cattle, except what I was able to pick up in a week's apprenticeship over in Jersey just before we sailed. My cattle enthusiasm has served its purpose, so I won't be needing it anymore. But thanks for the help getting those boys set up for our little party."

INTRODUCTION TO

THE WILD MAN INTERVIEWED

The following story was originally published September 18, 1869, in the Buffalo Express. It is not along the lines that you generally see reproduced from the pen of Mark Twain. It shows a much different side of Twain than the genial satirist that is generally portrayed. There is no humor here, and no redemption. And though including such a depressing story carries some risk, it also serves to underscore the range and depth of Twain's writings as well as their adaptability to today's world.

I found the idea of the story to be an equally compelling statement of current events as it was in Twain's time, so I borrowed heavily from the original in creating a new work that brings the concept into today's world. If you decide to tell a version of this story, I suggest that it be modified to include current events that you find compelling, infuriating, ironic or curious. From my perspective, this is the kind of story that benefits not only from the most current events, but also from describing things that are personally important to the storyteller at the moment. As such, it changes every time it is told.

THE WILD MAN INTERVIEWED

Adapted by Steve Daut,
Twain original first published in 1869

There's been so much talk about the mysterious "wild man" out there in the West for some time, that I finally felt it was my duty to go out and interview him. There was something touchingly romantic about the creature and his strange actions, according to the newspaper reports. He was represented as being hairy, long-armed, of great strength and stature, ugly and cumbersome. He was said to avoid men, but to appear suddenly and unexpectedly to women and children, although he never attacked any creature except to serve his need for sustenance. Further, he was portrayed as living in the woods like a wild beast and carrying a large wooden club. Accounts had him as inarticulate, never angry, but moaning and sometimes howling. I sought him out to try and understand the truth about him. I was surprised to find that, although he was dirty and unkempt, with heavy iron ringlets woven into his hair, he was articulate and attentive.

"Since you say you are a member of the press," said the wild man, "I'm willing to tell you all you wish to know, and you'll soon understand why. Although I have studiously avoided conversation with other people, I will now unfold my story."

"I am the son of Cain. I was present when the flood was announced. I am the father of the Tribes of Israel."

I moved out of range of his club and went on taking notes, but keeping a wary eye on him all the while. He smiled a melancholy smile and resumed:

"When I glance back over the dreary waste of ages, I remember much. Oh, the leagues I have traveled, the things I have seen! I was at the assassination of Caesar. I was in the Crusades, and have witnessed the beauty and brutality of all religions. I was in the Pinta's shrouds with Columbus when America burst upon his vision. I was in London when the Gunpowder Rebellion occurred. I was on American soil when the Declaration of Independence was written, when Cornwallis surrendered, when Washington died. In all the ages I have helped to celebrate the triumphs of genius, the achievements of arms, the havoc of storm, fire, pestilence, and famine."

I replied, "Your career has been a stirring one. Might I ask how you came to locate in these dull Kansas woods when you have been so accustomed to excitement during so much of history?"

He heaved a great sigh. "Once I was the honored servitor of the noble and illustrious, but in these degenerate days, I have become the slave of quack doctors, newspapers, and politicians. I have inhabited every privileged man who abuses and denigrates others to serve his egotistical need for power and wealth. I am the most recent politician who has sold his soul and the soul of America, to stay in office for one more term. I am the Las Vega shooter, the Paris bombers, the white supremacist, the child-abusing sports doctor, the masked terrorist executing his victim for the world to see, the latest socialite to indulge in a public divorce. I traffic in human flesh, lurk in the dark places just under the next street light, invade your home incessantly, and all to gratify the whim of frantic writers and to drive the wheels of media profit. From one end of the continent to the other, I am described as a beast, an animal. I serve the need for men to ask, 'How could such depravity exist in the human heart?', as they flip from pillar to post, seeking more and more of me."

"Mysterious being, a light begins to dawn. What —what is your name?"

"Sensation!"

A ringtone arose from a pocket in his clothes. He pulled out a cell phone and looked at it in horror.

"Oh pitiless fate, my destiny hounds me once more. I am called. I go. Alas, is there no rest for me?"

In a moment the wild man's features seemed to soften and refine, and his form to assume a more human grace and symmetry. Staring into the screen of his phone, he started away sighing profoundly and shedding tears.

"Where now, poor shadow?"

"To war!"

Such was the response that floated back upon the wind as the sad spirit shook its ringlets to the breeze and disappeared beyond the brow of the hill.

INTRODUCTION TO

THE FACTS IN THE GREAT LANDSLIDE CASE

This retelling is based on a version that was published in the *Buffalo Express* on April 2, 1870, which I initially discovered in a book entitled *Mark Twain at the Buffalo Express*. Endnotes in that book indicate that there were two previous versions, and a final version was included in Twain's book *Roughing It*, in 1872. Apparently, scholars believe that the story was probably based on an actual occurrence, although no record of the trial has been found.

As with many Twain stories, the original structure is somewhat problematic, but there is a classical struggle and resolution. Rather than reveal the secret as Twain does at the beginning, I feel the story is stronger by strategically repressing a bit of information in order to provide a surprise ending, although I drop a few hints along the way.

THE FACTS IN THE GREAT LANDSLIDE CASE

Adapted by Steve Daut,
Twain original first published in 1870

The mountains are very steep in the Nevada Territory, and during the Spring snowmelt, the earth can become saturated, causing it to liquefy, resulting in sudden and disastrous landslides. The whole side of a mountain can slide down into a valley, leaving a vast, treeless scar on the front of the mountain that lasts for years as a reminder of the catastrophic event.

Sometime around 1865, the Territorial officers in Nevada requested a United States Attorney, and the federal government's response was to ship out a man known as General Buncombe for the post. Buncombe considered himself to be a lawyer of sorts, and viewed the appointment as an opportunity to manifest his legal talents. Now, the older citizens of the territory looked upon outsiders with a non-malignant contempt, as long as they kept out of the way. When they began to think that an outsider such as Buncombe was getting in the way, they took steps to put that outsider in his place.

And so it was that one Spring morning Dick Sides rode furiously up to Buncombe's door in Carson City, demanding that the General defend him in a lawsuit, and if he won, Sides would pay him $500. Sides said it was pretty well known that he'd been farming successfully at the edge of a local valley for many years, and that Tom Morgan had a ranch just above it on the mountainside. And now, one of those dreaded landslides had come and slid Morgan's ranch, complete with intact fences, cabin, cattle, barns, and everything down on top of his ranch, covering up his entire spread to a depth of six feet. The problem was that Morgan rode down the mountain with his property, so was in possession, and refused to vacate the property. He said it was his own cabin and dirt, same as it always had been there, and there was no way he was going to vacate.

Sides wept as he described the scene of that mass of mud and vegetation rushing at him. "The whole world was tearing down and ripping up that mountainside, trees tumbling end over end, massive boulders rolling toward me. There were thick clouds of dust billowing out from the front and I thought it was the judgment coming to get me for sure. But once it settled down old Morgan stepped out from his cabin, declaring it had been quite a ride but he kind of liked his new location. When I told him he was sitting six foot on top of my property he told me that I gave up my right by vacating when I saw him coming."

"I didn't know what to do. I lost everything, and now old Morgan, who I thought was a friend of mine, was claiming I didn't have no right to the very land I had been working for years. I've been wandering around in the bush since then, and now I'm nearly starving and so mad I can't see straight. You wouldn't have a little something to eat, would you?"

Well, the General had never been so outraged in his life in hearing of Morgan's high-handed conduct. There was no way Morgan had any right to stay where he was. Morgan's claim was so outrageous that no lawyer would take his case and no judge would agree to hear it.

"That's what makes me even madder," said Sides. "I brought suit right here in Carson City, and Morgan already has a good local attorney to take the case. And a judge has accepted it. It's to be tried before a referee and ex-governor by the name of Roop."

This was the perfect opportunity for Buncombe to prove his mettle. He'd always suspected that the people of the Territory were fools, and now he knew it. The case was already won, and all he had to do was to settle down, look carefully at the laws involved and collect his witnesses. He sent Sides away with complete assurance of victory.

At 2 pm on the day of the hearing, referee Roop's court opened, and the old joker appeared to be enthroned among his sheriffs, the witnesses, and the general public. He uttered the command sternly: "Order in the court!"

The General elbowed his way through the crowd, his arms full of law books, and when the judge saw him, he issued the order. "Make way for the United States Attorney!"

This was the first respectful recognition of his high official dignity that the General had ever been honored with, and it saturated his whole system with pleasure.

The witnesses were called - legislators, high government officials, ranchers, miners, neighbors. Three-fourths of them were witnesses for the defendant Morgan, but every testimony went in favor of the plaintiff Sides. The Morgan lawyers made their speeches, which were stirring but hollow. Each word and phrase continued to point out the absurdity of claiming to own another man's property because his farm had slid down on top of it. Then the General made his case, confident in a stunning victory, based on the admiring countenances of everyone in the courtroom.

When he sat after his final argument, all eyes turned toward Ex-Governor Roop. The referee leaned his head upon his hand for several minutes, stood up, paced the floor beside the bench with long, deliberate strides, returned to his throne, and seated himself. Then the honorable Judge Roop cleared his throat and declared in his commanding voice:

"Gentlemen, a great responsibility rests upon me this day. This is no ordinary case, but the most solemn and awful that ever a man was called upon to decide. It is clear that the overwhelming weight of the evidence is in favor of the plaintiff Sides. Both attorneys have argued their cases credibly, and the law of man is clearly on the side of the plaintiff."

"On the other hand, we are merely worms in the eyes of Heaven, and it seems perfectly clear to me that Heaven, in its inscrutable wisdom, has seen fit to move this defendant's ranch for a reason. Gentlemen, it ill becomes us, worms as we are, to meddle with the decrees of Heaven. After all, Heaven created the ranches and it is Heaven's prerogative to rearrange them, experiment with them, and shift them around at its pleasure. It is hardly the province of men, worms as we are, to question the legality of the act. The sacrilegious brains and tongues of men must not meddle with such a divine act, and so it is the verdict of this court that the plaintiff, Richard Sides, has been deprived of his ranch by a visitation from God. And from this decision, there is no appeal!"

Buncombe seized his cargo of law books and plunged out of the courtroom, raving like a madman. He pronounced Roop to be a miraculous ass, a fool, and an inspired idiot. He spent the next few hours pacing in his quarters, screaming to high heaven and throwing things at nothing in particular. Finally, exhausted and weak from hunger, he went down the street to Baker's Tavern, only to find all of the occupants of the courtroom, including the defendant Tom Morgan and his own client Richard Sides, drinking and laughing together. When the door swung open, the bar went deathly silent. After a few moments, Ex-governor Roop stood solemnly, cleared his throat, and in that commanding voice of his, said:

"We were just taking bets on how long it would take you to realize that you have been a victim of an elaborate practical joke. Here, let me buy you a beer, and welcome, sir, to Carson City!"

The bar erupted in laughter and applause.

INTRODUCTION TO

RUNNING FOR GOVERNOR

This story was first published in the *Buffalo Express* on November 19, 1870. A book of Mark Twain stories would not be complete without including at least one that gives his take on political life. This is one of those stories that, ironically perhaps, gives me a great degree of hope that we will get by. Without putting too fine a point on it, there are so many echoes of the current state of politics in this story that I believe Twain has hit on a universal and timeless theme. It has always been thus in American politics.

It seems to me that one main difference between then and now is the speed of information dissemination. The early part of the 1800s was the era of the Penny Press – local newspapers that sold for a penny or two. From 1848 forward, these newspapers often shared information through the arrangement that would ultimately become the Associated Press newswire. The telegraph was invented in 1837 and the first Transatlantic telegraph cable was laid in 1866. By the time this story was published, even international news would be disseminated widely through the local papers. Some of these papers were dailies, but many were weeklies, and halftone technology (photographs reproduced in a matrix of dots) did not come into being until around 1880, so there were no photos in these newspapers. The result is that if a President, for instance, said something dumb, it would take at least a day, and generally more like a week before most Americans would hear about it. Today, of course, it takes seconds.

At any rate, if it's true that misery loves company, this seems to be a good story to keep in mind when people are feeling disgusted with politics. Historically, they are not alone. As with other Twain stories, I have added a few elements of struggle and conflict to round it out as a story.

RUNNING FOR GOVERNOR

Adapted by Steve Daut,
Twain original first published in 1870

A few months ago I was nominated for Governor of the great state of New York as an independent, to run against the two-party candidates. I somehow felt that I had one prominent advantage over these gentlemen, and that was good character. It was easy to see by the newspapers that, if ever the other two candidates had known what it was to bear a good name, that time had gone by. In these latter years they had both become familiar with all manner of shameful crimes.

But though I felt honored and flattered at the nomination, I was also disturbed by having to hear my name bandied about in familiar connection with such people. I grew more and more disturbed. Finally, I wrote my grandmother about it, and her answer came quick and sharp. She said, "You have never done one single thing in all your life to be ashamed of. You must look at what the newspapers say about the other candidates and decide if you're willing to lower yourself to their level and enter the public spotlight with them." This was my very same thought! But I was fully committed and decided I must go on with the fight.

The next morning I was looking over the papers at breakfast, and I came across this paragraph: "Perhaps, now that Mr. Mark Twain is a candidate for Governor, he'll explain how he came to be convicted of perjury by thirty-four witnesses in Cochin China in 1863, with the intent of stealing a plantain patch from a poor native widow and her helpless family. This meager property was the family's only support against total desolation. Mr. Twain owes it to the voters to clear this matter up. Will he do it?"

I never had seen Cochin China! I didn't know a plantain patch from a kangaroo! I didn't know what to do. I was crazed and helpless, and let the day slip away without doing anything at all about it.

The next morning the same paper had this: "Mr. Twain is suggestively silent about the Cochin China perjury." The article kept referring to me as "the Infamous Perjurer Twain."

Next came the *Gazette* with this: "Will the new candidate for Governor explain to his fellow citizens how it was that his cabin-mates in Montana began losing small valuables from time to time, until at last, these things were found in Mr. Twain's possession? His cabin-mates reportedly gave him a friendly admonition for his own good, then tarred and feathered him, and advised him to leave a permanent vacuum in the place he usually occupied in the camp." After this, this journal customarily spoke of me as, "Twain, the Montana Thief'."

Could anything be more deliberately malicious than that? I never was in Montana in my life.

I got to picking up papers apprehensively, much as you might lift a blanket if you suspected it might have a rattlesnake under it.

One day this met my eye: "By the sworn affidavits of trusted local attorneys, Mr. Mark Twain lied when he made the vile statement that the grandfather of our most noble citizen, Blank J. Blank, was hanged for highway robbery. This is a brutal and gratuitous lie, without a shadow of foundation in fact. It's disheartening to see Twain resort to seek political gain by such shameful means as attacking the dead in their graves and defiling their honored names with slander. This is such a vile deed that if passion should get the better of an outraged and insulted public, and in its blind fury they should do Twain bodily injury, it's obvious that no jury would convict and no court would punish the perpetrators of the deed."

The ingenious closing sentence had the effect of moving me out of bed with dispatch that night, and out the back door also, while the "outraged and insulted public" surged in the front way, breaking furniture and windows in their righteous indignation. They departed with such property as they could carry when they left. And yet I can lay my hand upon the Book and say that I never slandered Mr. Blank's grandfather. In fact, I had never even heard of him or mentioned him up to that day. The label they applied: "Twain, the Body-Snatcher."

The next newspaper article that attracted my attention was the following: "Twain's physician sent a telegram indicating that the reason he didn't deliver his speech to the mass-meeting of the Independents last night, was that a runaway train had knocked him down and broken his leg in two places. We have reason to suspect otherwise. A certain man was seen to reel into Mr. Twain's hotel last night in a state of beastly intoxication. It is the imperative duty of the Independents to prove that this besotted brute was not Mark Twain himself. The voice of the people demands in thunder tones, to know who that man was."

It was incredible, absolutely incredible, that my name was coupled with this disgraceful suspicion. Three years had passed since I had tasted ale, beer, wine or liquor or any kind. Yet it didn't stop the paper from dubbing me "Mr. Delirium Tremens Twain".

By this time anonymous letters were an important part of my mail. Some snippets: "How about that old beggar woman you kicked off your premises? I know some terrible secrets about you that I'll share with the papers unless you send a few unmarked bills to the following address" and so forth. I could continue this list indefinitely, but you get the idea.

Soon the principal Republican journal convicted me of wholesale bribery, and the leading Democratic paper accused me of a case of aggravated blackmailing. In this way I acquired two additional names: "Twain the Filthy Corruptionist" and "Twain the Loathsome Embracer."

By this time there had grown to be such a clamor for an "answer" to all the dreadful charges that were laid to me that the leaders of my party said it would be political ruin for me to remain silent any longer. As if to make their appeal more imperative, the following appeared in one of the papers the very next day:

"Mark Twain, the independent candidate, still maintains silence because he dare not speak. Every accusation against him has been amply proved, and they have been confirmed by his own eloquent silence, till he stands forever convicted. Look upon your candidate, Independents! Look upon the Infamous Perjurer! the Montana Thief! the Body-Snatcher! Contemplate your incarnate Delirium Tremens! your Filthy Corruptionist! your Loathsome Embracer! Gaze upon him, ponder him well, and then say if you can give your honest votes to a creature who has earned this dismal array of titles by his hideous crimes, and dares not open his mouth in denial of any one of them!"

There was no possible way of getting out of it, and so, in deep humiliation, I set about preparing to answer a mass of baseless charges and mean and wicked falsehoods. But I never finished the task, for the very next morning a paper came out with a new horror, a fresh malignancy, and charged me with burning a lunatic asylum with all its inmates because it obstructed the view from my house. Then came the charge of me poisoning my uncle to get his property, with an imperative demand that the grave should be opened. On top of this, I was accused of employing toothless and incompetent relatives to prepare the food for a hospital filled with abandoned children.

I was wavering, wavering. At last, as a due and fitting climax to the shameless persecution that party rancor had inflicted upon me, nine little toddling children, of all shades of color and degrees of raggedness, were taught to rush onto the platform at public meetings, clasp me around the legs, and call me Daddy! I gave it up. I hauled down my colors and surrendered. I was not equal to the requirements of a Gubernatorial campaign in the state of New York, and so I sent in my withdrawal from the candidacy. In bitterness of spirit, I signed it, "Truly yours, once a decent man, but now Mark Twain, perjurer, thief, body snatcher, hopeless drunk and all-around sociopath."

INTRODUCTION TO

A MEDIEVAL ROMANCE

This story is another departure for Twain, who was, of course, naturally prone to departures. It begins with the appearance of a typical convoluted European folktale and takes a twist at the end that is pure Twain. In fact, with the right audience, this can be set up as a great "gotcha" story.

Early on, this story was entitled *Awful, Terrible Medieval Romance*. The original story runs to around 3,000 words and is divided into 5 sections. This version is a little over one-third of that, and can be told in around 13 minutes.

A MEDIEVAL ROMANCE

Adapted by Steve Daut,
Twain original first published in 1870

One windswept evening in the year 1222, in the feudal castle of Klugenstein, a secret council was held between the Lord of Klugenstein and his daughter, who had been named Conrad and raised as a young man of noble presence. "Daughter," the old lord said, "the time has come to tell you why your true gender has been hidden from the world. My brother Ulrich is the great Duke of Brandenburg. On his deathbed, our father decreed that if no son was born to Ulrich but one was born to me, the throne would pass to my son. If only daughters were born to both of us, Ulrich's daughter would ascend to the throne. So all who witnessed your birth were put to death, except your mother, of course. Ulrich has only a daughter, so the throne is yours for the taking. Since he has become as feeble as I, he has asked that you come to him right away and become Duke, in act, though not yet in name. You leave tonight."

"Now listen well, and remember every word I say. There is a law as old as the earth, that if any woman sits for a single instant in the ducal throne before she has been crowned in the presence of the people, she shall die. So listen close.

Pretend humility; pronounce your judgments from the foot of the throne, not from the throne itself. Your sex may never be discovered, but if it is, your power is safe after you have been crowned. But if you violate this ancient law, nothing can save you from a horrible death."

Though Conrad had misgivings about this terrible deception, he (or she) set off with his retinue for the Duchy of Brandenburgh and was welcomed with open arms by Ulrich and his court. But in a remote apartment of Brandenburgh castle, Ulrich's only daughter, Constance, was weeping. Her secret lover, hearing of Conrad's arrival, had fled for fear that with all of the changes that were bound to occur, their illicit affair would be discovered. Ulrich was sure to plan a horrible death for the lad, since he had told the low-born boy more than once to stay far away from the Lady Constance. Her lover's departure, of course, left Lady Constance bereft, and lonely.

Ulrich's heart was filled with happiness, because he loved Conrad as soon as he set eyes on the young heir. A few months drifted by, and Conrad began to win the favor of Ulrich and all the people of Brandenburg. The old Duke soon gave everything into Conrad's hands, sitting apart and listening with proud satisfaction as his heir delivered decrees from in front of the throne.

But here the plot thickens. Conrad began to catch the rapt attention of Lady Constance, who was desperate to fill the hole in her heart. Conrad welcomed this attention because he needed all the allies he could get in order to be crowned quickly before his deception was discovered. And secretly, he longed for the comfort and companionship of another woman, for the sympathy and support that only a woman can give. This apparent romance pleased Ulrich greatly, for a pairing of these two would unite the kingdom. But the girl began to haunt Conrad, to hunt him, in all places, night and day. The princess had begun to love him. He tried to avoid her, but she persisted. Finally, one night she came upon him in an abandoned hallway and flung her arms around his neck so he could not escape her. She said, "Why do you avoid me? We were becoming such good friends and now you run from me. But you can avoid me no longer. I love you, Conrad, and you will love me as well!"

Conrad ripped her arms from around his neck and cried, "You don't know what you're asking. It is forever and ever impossible." He fled, devastated, and the poor girl stood in stunned amazement. The second rejection in only a few months drove Constance out of her mind. Her anger boiled within her. "To think he was despising my love at the very moment I thought it was melting his cruel heart! He spurned me like a dog! How I hate him!" She would surely find a way to have her revenge.

Conrad continued to grow in favor, and his confidence and wisdom grew. But the Lady Constance was nowhere to be seen. Soon, a rumor swept the kingdom and all the way back to Klugenstein, a rumor that Constance had given birth to a child. Conrad's father rejoiced in the news, knowing that since Ulrich's daughter had brought such shame on herself, the coronation of Conrad would proceed apace. He departed for Brandenburg to attend the trial of the princess in order to watch Conrad's moment of final triumph.

As acting Duke, it fell to Conrad to conduct the trial of Constance. He begged to be relieved of the duty, but this was his test of fitness for the throne. He could not refuse. All the great lords and barons of Brandenburg were assembled in the palace. The Prisoner, Constance, was called forth. The Lord Chief Justice declared that the penalty for giving birth out of wedlock, by ancient law, was death, unless she delivered up the father of the child to the executioner. It fell to Conrad to give that sentence. Reluctantly, Conrad stood at the base of the throne and stretched forth his scepter, while at the same time his womanly heart yearned in pity toward the doomed prisoner. The Chief justice stopped him and said, "Not there, your Grace. It is not lawful to pronounce judgment on any of royal blood except from the ducal throne!" But Conrad had not been crowned. The words of his father returned to him. "If any woman sits for a single instant in the ducal chair before she has been crowned in the presence of the people, she shall die."

Yet he ascended the throne and made the required pronouncement. His eyes met those of Constance and he pleaded with her. "The ancient law provides an opportunity to save you from death. Deliver up the name of the father for execution and you will be spared."

Her eyes burned with hatred and she declared, "It is you! You are the father of my child!"

What could Conrad do? He could prove it was not him by revealing himself to be a woman, on penalty of death. Or he could remain silent on penalty of death. At one and the same moment, he and his grim old father swooned and fell to the ground.

Well, it's a perplexing dilemma. The truth is, I have got my hero (or heroine) into such a particularly close place that I don't see how I am ever going to get him (or her) out of it again, and therefore I wash my hands of the whole business. I thought it was going to be easy to straighten out that little difficulty, but it looks impossible now.

INTRODUCTION TO

SOME LEARNED FABLES FOR GOOD OLD BOYS AND GIRLS

This is one of many Twain fables that is written in multiple parts.

This fable is of intense interest to me, because it seems almost like a good science fiction story, predicting things to come. Twain also gores a venerated ox that forms the foundation of my geological training. He invokes The Old Red Sandstone, a formation that was first discovered in Scotland and named by James Hutton, founding father of geology. To make light of it seems, well, almost sacrilegious. I'm sure that's what Twain had in mind.

This story appears to predict the ideas of Thomas S. Kuhn, an American physicist, historian, and philosopher of science who wrote a controversial book, originally published in 1962, entitled *The Structure of Scientific Revolutions*. Kuhn's assertion in the book is that science is moved forward, not by steadily adding to knowledge and correcting itself as new discoveries are made, but in fits and starts. Specifically, he says that most scientific effort is spent trying to prop up and add details to the accepted theories of the time. Although scientist may think they are making new discoveries, if anything contradicts the traditional theories of the time, it is regarded as an anomaly, an outlier that must be due to poor method or faulty equipment.

If someone comes along who is not one of the venerated establishment, they are shuffled aside and considered misguided, uninformed, or just plain crazy. It is only after the nonconforming discoveries become too large and insistent to ignore that the revolution begins, and ushers in a new scientific paradigm. This, says Kuhn, is what happened when Einstein proposed his Theory of Relativity, and when Quantum Theory was born.

In this story, then, the scientific expedition is dominated by the venerated establishment, and Tumble-Bug is in the unfortunate position of embodying the first stirrings of revolution. This story should be considered a tragedy then, because we, as the audience, can see the errors that are being made by the established scientists, but Tumble-Bug never is able to convince them of their folly. Finally, he retreats before blind science and the unquestioning faith of religion. We can only hope that the seeds of revolution begin to bear fruit after this story ends.

The main challenge with telling this story is in walking the line between seeing things the way the creatures see them and giving enough hints for the audience to determine what they actually are. I'll admit that I struggled for a long time trying to figure out what the "hard smooth object . . . plugged by a woody object" was, until my wife figured it out. With a written story, you can always go back and puzzle over it, but it needs to be pretty clear in the telling. So this story took a fair amount of revision to convert it into something that works in oral presentation. It's also very long, so is generally easier to read than to tell. Either way, I think it's worth the effort because it provides a lot of opportunities to create interesting characters and voices.

SOME LEARNED FABLES FOR GOOD OLD BOYS AND GIRLS

Adapted by Steve Daut,
Twain original first published in 1875

Once upon a time the creatures of the forest held a great convention and appointed a commission consisting of the most illustrious scientists among them to go forth, beyond the forest, and into the unknown and unexplored world, to verify the truth of the matters already taught in their schools and colleges, and also to make new discoveries. It was the most imposing enterprise that the nation had ever begun.

True, the government had once sent Dr. Bull Frog and his crew to hunt for a northwesterly passage through the swamp, and had since sent out many expeditions to hunt for Dr. Bull Frog. But they never could find him. And once, the government sent Sir Grass Hopper to hunt for the source of the stream that emptied into the swamp. Later they found his body. If he had discovered the source of the stream, he did not let on.

But these expeditions were trifles compared with the present one, for this one was comprised of the very greatest among the scholars to visit utterly unvisited regions believed to lie beyond the mighty forest.

They set off, and it was a sight to see the long procession of dry-land tortoises heavily laden with savants, scientific instruments, glow-worms and fire-flies for signal service, provisions, ants and tumble-bugs to fetch and carry and delve, spiders to carry the surveying chain and conduct other engineering duties. After the tortoises, came a long train of ironclad mud turtles for marine transportation service. From every tortoise and turtle flew a splendid banner. At the head of the column, a great band of bumble-bees, mosquitoes, katydids, and crickets played marching music. The entire train was escorted by twelve picked regiments of the armyworm.

At the end of three weeks, the expedition emerged from the forest. A vast level plain stretched before them, watered by a sinuous stream, and beyond, there towered a lofty barrier of some kind. Tumble-Bug said he believed it was simply land tilted up on its edge, because he could see trees on it.

Professor Snail and the others said, "You are hired to dig, sir, that is all. We need your muscle, not your brains. When we want your opinion on scientific matters, we will let you know. Why are you even here, meddling with august matters of learning, when the other laborers are pitching camp? Go along and help handle the baggage."

Tumble-Bug turned on his heel uncrushed, unabashed, observing to himself, "If it isn't land tilted up, let me die the death of the unrighteous."

Professor Bull Frog said he believed the ridge was the wall that enclosed the earth. He continued, "Our fathers did not travel this far, and so we may count this a noble new discovery. But I wonder what this wall is built of?"

Professor Snail adjusted his field-glass and examined the rampart critically. Finally he said, "The thing is obvious. It's a dense vapor of some sort."

"Profound mind!" said Professor Angle-Worm, "Nothing can long remain a mystery to that majestic brain."

After breakfast in the morning, the expedition moved on. About noon a great avenue was reached, which had in it two endless parallel bars that stood two frog-heights above the rocky substrate and were made of some hard red-brown substance, but shiny on top. The scientists climbed up on these and examined and tested them in various ways but they could arrive at no decision. There was nothing in the records of science that mentioned anything of this kind.

At last the venerable geographer, Professor Mud Turtle, proclaimed, "My friends, we have indeed made a discovery here. Humble yourselves, my friends, for we stand in a majestic presence. These are parallels of latitude!" Every heart and every head was bowed and many tears were shed, so sublime was the magnitude of the discovery. The rest of the day was spent writing voluminous accounts of the marvel, and correcting astronomical tables to fit it.

Meanwhile, Tumble-Bug thought to himself that the bars looked like some sort of track for a large moving machine of some kind. But he kept to himself because he knew they would not listen to him.

Toward midnight a demoniacal shriek was heard, then a clattering and rumbling noise, and the next instant a vast terrific eye shone brightly through the dark, seemingly anchored to those two parallel bars. It shot by, with a long segmented tail attached, and disappeared in the gloom, still uttering triumphant shrieks. The laborers were stricken to the heart with fright, but not the scientists. They calmly proceeded to exchange theories.

Professor Mud Turtle went into his shell and deliberated long and profoundly. Finally, he emerged and pronounced, "Give thanks for this stupendous thing which we have been permitted to witness. It is the Vernal Equinox!"

"But," said Angle-Worm, uncoiling after reflection, "this is dead summer-time. And besides, how can the sun pass in the night?"

"Very well," said Turtle, "The season and time of day differ with the difference of time between our region and this." Though no one understood what this meant, they accepted the explanation as preferable to sounding ignorant by asking an impertinent question.

But about this moment that dreadful shrieking was heard

again. Again the rumbling and thundering came speeding up out of the night. But this time the flaming great eye came along those bars in exactly the opposite direction as the first. The wrinkled and withered Professor Woodlouse spoke up. "Perhaps I ought not to presume to meddle with matters pertaining to astronomy at all, but as this last apparition proceeded in exactly the opposite direction from the first, which you decided to be the Vernal Equinox, is it not possible that it was the Autumnal Equinox?"

Lord Daddy Longlegs responded. "It is correct that you should not meddle with my area of expertise, as what you suggest is preposterous. Nay, my fellow-scientists, it is my belief that we have witnessed a thing which has occurred only once before in the knowledge of created beings. The great marvel that we have just witnessed is nothing less than the transit of Venus! If you are inclined to disagree that such a thing could occur, I offer the best possible proof. We have just seen it!"

Every scholar sprang to his feet pale with astonishment. Then ensued tears, handshaking, frenzied embraces, and the most extravagant jubilations of every sort.

In the commotion, Tumble-Bug had just intruded, unnoticed. He came reeling forward among the scholars, congratulating them on their profound discovery, while still secretly wondering at their conclusions. When it was discovered that he was mingling with the venerable scientists, acting as if he was their equal, the scholarly euphoria stopped abruptly, and

Professor Bull Frog roared out, "No more of this, sir Tumble-Bug! Say your say and then get you about your business with speed! Quick, what is your errand? And back away before you tell it. You smell like a stable."

"Please your worship," said Tumble-Bug. "I have chanced upon a find."

The commission went together to view the find. It was found to consist of a hard, smooth, nearly transparent object with a rounded summit surmounted by a short upright projection resembling a section of a cabbage stalk divided transversely. This projection was not solid, but was a hollow cylinder plugged with a soft woody substance unknown to our region. Norway Rat was recruited to nibble away at the plug and finally remove it. The object was found to be nearly filled with a pungent liquid of a brownish hue, like rainwater that has stood for some time. Norway Rat engaged in thrusting his tail into the cylindrical projection, drawing it out dripping, permitting the struggling multitude of laborers to suck the end of it, then straightway reinserting it and delivering the fluid to the mob as before.

Evidently this liquor had strangely potent qualities, for all that partook of it were immediately exalted with great and pleasurable emotions, and went staggering about singing ribald songs, embracing, fighting, dancing, erupting in profanity, and defying all authority. The elite and illustrious academics were soon drawn into the fray and the camp wore itself out with its orgies, then sank into a stolid and pitiable stupor. Rank was forgotten and strange bedfellows made. By the next morning, all eyes were blasted and all souls petrified with the incredible spectacle of that intolerable stinking scavenger, Tumble-Bug, and the illustrious patrician Lord Grand Daddy, Duke of Longlegs, lying soundly steeped together in sleep. Something had to be done.

With no delay, engineer-in-chief Herr Spider had his crew rig the necessary tackle to overturn the vast reservoir, and so its intoxicating contents were discharged in a torrent upon the thirsty earth. Then there was no more danger, except a few drops reserved for experiment and scrutiny. It's been determined that the substance is, without question, that fierce and most destructive fluid called lightning. The container was apparently pulled from its storehouse in the clouds by the resistless might of the flying planet, and hurled at our feet as she sped by.

Some days later Professor Bull Frog discovered a strange tree and called his comrades. It was very tall and straight, and wholly devoid of bark, limbs, or foliage. After additional exploration it was found that there were a great number of these trees, extending in a single rank, with wide intervals between, all bound together near their tops by fourteen great ropes, continuous from tree to tree, as far as his vision reached. Chief Engineer Spider ran aloft and soon reported that these ropes were simply a web hung there by some colossal member of his own species, for he could see its prey dangling here and there from the strands. Then he ran along one of the ropes to make a closer inspection, but felt a smart sudden burn on the soles of his feet, accompanied by a paralyzing shock, wherefore he let go and swung himself to earth by a thread of his own spinning, and advised all to hurry to camp, lest the monster should appear and become interested in members of the expedition.

That evening the naturalist built a beautiful model of the colossal spider, having no need to see it in order to do this, because he had picked up a fragment of its vertebra by the tree, and so knew exactly what the creature looked like and what its habits and its preferences were by this simple evidence alone. He built it with a tail, teeth, fourteen legs, and a snout, and said it ate grass, cattle, pebbles, and dirt with equal enthusiasm. This animal was regarded as a very precious addition to science, and was named after the naturalist, since he, after God, had created it. "And improved it, mayhap," muttered Tumble-Bug, who was intruding again, according to his idle custom and his unappeasable curiosity.

A week later the expedition encountered a collection of stone caverns that stood in long, straight rows. The summit of each cavern sloped sharply both ways, and several horizontal rows of great square holes, obstructed by a thin, shiny, transparent substance, pierced the frontage and sides of each cavern. There were many huge, shapeless objects inside each cavern that were once living creatures, as they were covered with loose, dry skin. And there were strange smallish trees, rootless, with four trunks, large flat tops, and no leaves at all.

After close examination of the caverns, the scientists determined that these formations belonged mainly to the Old Red Sandstone period. The cavern fronts rose in innumerable and wonderfully regular strata high in the air, each stratum about five frog-spans thick. In the present discovery lay an overpowering refutation of all received geology, for by a careful examination of the layering of decomposed limestone and other unrecognizable materials, it was plain that there had been a hundred and seventy-five floodings of the earth, each flooding depositing a layer of limestone strata. The unavoidable deduction was the overwhelming truth that the world, instead of being only two hundred thousand years old, was older by millions upon millions of years!

A critical examination of some of the lower strata demonstrated the presence of fossil ants and tumble-bugs, and this gratifying fact was enrolled upon the scientific record as proof that these vulgar laborers belonged to the first and lowest orders of created beings. It was, however, repulsive to reflect that the perfect and exquisite creature of the modern uppermost order owed its origin to such ignominious beings through the mysterious law of Development of Species.

Tumble-Bug, overhearing this discussion, said the higher order creature might as well find comfort in their laws and theories, as he was content to be of the old first families and proud to point back to his place among the original aristocracy of the land. He said, "Enjoy your mushroom dignity, stinking of yesterday's varnish. It's sufficient for the race of Tumble-Bugs to know that untold generations of forebears rolled their fragrant spheres down the solemn aisles of antiquity and left their imperishable works embalmed in the Old Red Sandstone!"

"Oh, take a walk!" said the chief of the expedition, with derision.

The summer passed, and winter approached. In many of the caverns were what seemed to be inscriptions. Professor Woodlouse undertook to decipher these inscriptions, following the classical scientific method. That is to say, he placed a number of copies of inscriptions in front of him and studied them both collectively and in detail.

To begin with, he placed the following copies together: The American Hotel, Meals at All Hours, NO SMOKING, Boats for Hire Cheap, Union Prayer Meeting 6 pm, A1 Barber Shop, Billiards, The Waterside Journal, Brandith's Pills – A Cure for All that Ails You. His examination revealed that it was a language which conveyed itself partly by letters, and partly by signs or hieroglyphics. By noting formations that occurred more frequently than others, he was able to piece together a rudimentary understanding of this language. Finally, a cavern was discovered with these inscriptions upon it: Waterside Museum. Open at All Hours. Wonderful Collection of Wax Works, fossils, and more.

Professor Woodlouse affirmed that the word "Museum" was equivalent to the phrase "lumgath molo," or "Burial Place." Upon entering, the scientists encountered a row of massive, rigid figures which most certainly belonged to the long extinct species of reptile called Man. This was a gratifying discovery because Man was generally regarded as a myth and a superstition.

But here, indeed, was Man, perfectly preserved in a fossil state. And these were obviously venerated members of the species, since each was preserved in an upright posture, and upon each breast was an inscription. One read, "Captain Kidd the Pirate," another, "Queen Victoria," another, "Abe Lincoln." There were many such fossils.

In order to confirm that these creatures were, indeed, the species called Man, Professor Woodlouse consulted the records that he had brought with him from the archives. He read as follows:

"In the time of our fathers, Man still walked the earth. It was a creature of exceeding great size, being compassed about with a loose skin, sometimes of one color, sometimes of many. The hind legs were armed with short claws like a mole's but broader, and the forelegs had fingers of a curious slimness and a length much longer than a frog's. It had a sort of feathers upon its head such as a rat, but longer, and a beak suitable for seeking its food by scent. When it was stirred with happiness, it leaked water from its eyes, and when it suffered or was sad, it manifested a horrible hellish cackling clamor that was exceeding dreadful to hear. Two Mans together uttered noises at each other like this: "Haw-haw-haw, good joke, good joke."

We found many more things in this burial place, confirming

that though some details would need to be revised, this indeed was a place of Man as described in our archives. We believe that Man was the companion of the cave-bear, the mastodon, and other extinct species, that he cooked and ate them and likewise ate the young of his own kind, that he bore rude weapons and knew something of art, that he imagined he had a soul, and pleased himself with the fancy that it was immortal. But let us not laugh. There may be creatures in existence to whom we and our vanities may seem as ludicrous.

Many more inscriptions were found, and with infinite trouble, Professor Woodlouse succeeded in making a translation of the inscriptions, piecing together the language with some clarity. At one point there was found a huge, shapely stone which appeared to be a chronicle of some dwelling place that was called a "city," and contained most prominently the word "Mayor." According to Professor Woodlouse, "Mayor" is best translated as "King," and the stone has been dubbed the "Mayoritish Stone" which of course is but another way of saying "King Stone." This achievement gave the good Professor such a reputation that at once every seat of learning in his native land conferred a degree of the most illustrious grade upon him. This beginning was the origin of that school of scientists called Manologists, whose specialty is deciphering the ancient records of the extinct bird termed Man. For it is now determined that Man was a bird and not a reptile.

The growing rigor of the weather drove the scientists to close their labors for the present, so they made preparations to journey homeward. But even their last day among the Caverns bore fruit, for one of the scholars found in an out-of-the-way corner of the Museum or "Burial Place" an inscription that Professor Woodlouse translated to reveal the following sentence: "In truth, it is believed by many that the lower animals reason and talk together."

It was the most startling discovery yet, for it must mean that there are lower animals even than Man! The enthusiasm of the scientists burst all bounds in anticipation of the brilliant field of discovery and investigation here thrown open to science. All of the assembled scholars agreed to petition the government for research into the discovery of this hitherto unsuspected race of creatures.

The expedition then journeyed homeward after its long absence and its faithful endeavors, and was received with a mighty ovation by the whole grateful country. There were vulgar, ignorant carpers, of course, as there always are and always will be. Naturally one of these was the obscene Tumble-Bug.

He said that all he had learned by his travels was that science only needed a spoonful of supposition to build a mountain of demonstrated fact, and for the future he meant to be content with the meager knowledge that nature had made free to all creatures. He vowed never again to go prying into the deeper secrets of the Deity.

INTRODUCTION TO

ONE LITTLE TALE

I have actually renamed this story, as it is an excerpt from a story titled *Two Little Tales*. The original is a tale within a tale, but it seemed to me that the "outer" tale that wraps around this one doesn't really contribute anything to the underlying story, so I got rid of it and I just tell the "inner" story. I have also given it a fairy-tale ending, as that's what it seems to deserve.

Historically, it looks like the premise of this story may be accurate. In the 1700's and 1800's, doctors treated dysentery with laudanum, large doses of water, and even laxatives. Many thought one cause of the malady was eating raw fruit, so it would make sense that watermelon was banned, yet today it is considered to be an effective natural cure.

ONE LITTLE TALE

Adapted by Steve Daut,
Twain original first published in 1901

It was summer, and even the strong were suffering under the awful heat. The army was wasting away from dysentery, and even the medication that they had was no longer working. The Emperor summoned the physicians to him and called them to account. If they knew their craft, why were the soldiers dying? Could it be that they were not proper healers and didn't know their craft, or could it be that they were assassins?

The oldest doctor of them all stepped forward and said, "We have done what we could, your Majesty, but no medicine can cure this disease, only nature and a good constitution can do it. Sometimes we can only try our best to help nature, but there is little help that we can offer."

The Emperor, being a profane and passionate man, drove the physicians from his presence. Within a day, he was attacked by the disease himself, and the word of his illness went out throughout the land. This resulted in a general depression, for few had any hope for his recovery.

In a remote and lowly part of the empire lived Tommy, a bright lad of sixteen. Tommy's father emptied cesspools and drove a night-cart, collecting excrement for disposal. Tommy's closest friend was Jimmy, the chimney sweep. Jimmy was fourteen and a slim little fellow with a good heart who was honest and industrious. Jimmy went home every night and emptied out his boots, for they had long since worn out, and the black ashes from the chimneys he swept would creep into them through all of the holes. One day after their labors, Jimmy and Tommy sat down on the curbstone to talk. The subject of the Emperor's malady came up, and Jimmy said that he knew how to cure it.

In surprise, Tommy said, "What? You? Why you little fool. Even the best doctors can't cure him."

"I give you my word that I could cure him in fifteen minutes."

Tommy looked at Jimmy for a long time. "I believe you're serious, Jimmy. What is this miracle cure?"

"Just tell him to eat a slice of raw watermelon."

This caught Tommy rather suddenly, and he howled with laughter. Then he saw that his dear friend was hurt by his derision and he sobered up the best he could. "I'm sorry," he said. "I didn't mean any harm, and I won't do it again. It just seemed funny, because wherever there's a soldiers' camp and dysentery, the doctors always put up a sign saying anyone caught bringing watermelons there will be severely beaten."

Jimmy had tears in his eyes as he said, "I know. They're not only quacks, but think of all those men who died when they didn't need to."

"But where did you get such a notion?"

"I've watched the old Zulu do it, the one with gray hair who's friends with my mother. He's been curing people for years. It only takes one or two slices of melon and it doesn't matter how long they've had the disease. It will cure it."

"Ok, let's agree that it does work. Do you know the Emperor? Are you just going to walk up to him and tell him to eat some watermelon?"

"Of course not."

"Then how are you going to tell him?"

Well, this was a dilemma. The boys talked and talked about it. At first, they thought they would send him a letter, but realized that everyone in the empire would be sending him letters, and he'd probably pay more attention to the smooth-talking quacks than any real advice. And if they tried to tell high-born strangers, none of them would believe it. So what they decided to do was to tell only their friends who trusted them. Then all of those people also told those who trusted them, and so on. Eventually, the word got all the way up to the Emperor, who ate some watermelon and was cured.

The Emperor ordered that this source of this miracle cure be discovered, so his investigators traced backward across all of the people who had passed this information along, and eventually it got back to little Jimmy, the chimney-sweep. And the very next morning, a royal carriage drove down the narrow streets of that lowly neighborhood. It stopped at Jimmy's house, and with great fanfare, the Emperor emerged and went in to see Jimmy.

"Young man," he said. "You alone, among all of my empire, have saved my life. Name your price, for my gratitude knows no bounds."

It took Jimmy only a moment to reply. "All I need for myself, your Majesty, is a pair of boots, for it was not only me who saved your life. It was all of the people who kept the faith and passed the message on to you. But for the soldiers, I ask that you provide the same cure to them as you took for yourself."

Before the day was out, the "no watermelon" signs were gone, carriage loads of watermelons were delivered to all the soldier camps, and Jimmy had a shiny new pair of the finest boots money could buy.

THE FIVE BOONS OF LIFE

I debated for a long time before including this strange little tale, because like *The Wild Man Interviewed*, it seems deeply pessimistic for Twain. There is no redemption here, as the tale claims all is impermanence except death, and views old age as a wanton insult. But after some consideration, I decided to take a look at what was going on in Twain's life at the time, and saw that this story was written around the time that Twain's wife, Olivia Langdon Clemens, was diagnosed with serious illness. The doctors advised her to avoid becoming overly agitated and therefore to keep a distance from her husband. Following this advice, she began to go for months without seeing him. It is no wonder that, during that period, Twain considered the process of aging to be a wanton insult. Livy, as he called his wife, died two years later of heart failure after being married to Twain for 34 years.

Although entitled *The Five Boons of Life*, it is really about the five ages of life, and really seems to parallel Twain's life. As such it can be seen as a very concise autobiography. He was working on his full-length autobiography at the time and two years later, after Livy died, he began to focus full time on that longer work. But as it provides a rare glimpse into the mindset of the man behind the Mark Twain character, I decided to include it here.

The story is tightly written in its original form, so less editing was necessary than in other stories. I have made one major change in the tone of the piece by changing the ending, eliminating the final exchange between Twain and the fairy and emphasizing his failure to ask for the fairy's judgment. It seems to me more powerful (and less pessimistic) to leave out this exchange, which is in the original is as follows:

Twain says: "Oh, miserable me! What is left for me?"

The fairy replies: "What not even you have deserved: the wanton insult of Old Age."

THE FIVE BOONS OF LIFE

Adapted by Steve Daut,
Twain original first published in 1902

In the morning of life came a good fairy with her basket, and said: "Here are gifts. Take one, leave the others. And be wary, chose wisely, for only one of them is valuable." The gifts were five: Fame, Love, Riches, Pleasure, and Death.

The youth said, eagerly, "There is no need to consider."

He chose Pleasure. He went out into the world and sought out the pleasures that youth delights in. But each in its turn was short-lived and disappointing, vain and empty, and each, departing, mocked him. In the end, he said, "I have wasted these first years. If I could but choose again, I would choose wisely."

Then the fairy appeared again, and said, "Four of the gifts remain. Choose once more, and remember, only one of them is precious."

The man considered long, then chose Love. He did not mark the tears that rose in the fairy's eyes. After many years, the man sat by a coffin, in an empty home. And he communed with himself, saying, "One by one they have gone away and left me. Now she lies here, the dearest and the last. Desolation after desolation has swept over me. I have paid a thousand hours of grief for each hour of happiness the treacherous trader, Love, has sold me. Out of my heart of hearts, I curse him."

The fairy appeared and spoke once more. "Choose again. The years have surely taught you wisdom by now. Three gifts remain. Remember that only one of them has any worth, and choose warily."

The man reflected long, then chose Fame. The fairy, sighing, went her way. Years went by and she came again, and stood behind the man where he sat solitary in the fading day, thinking. And she knew his thought. "My name filled the world, and its praises were on every tongue, and it seemed well with me for a little while. How little a while it was! Then came envy, then detraction, then defamation, then hate, then persecution. Then derision, which is the beginning of the end. And last of all came pity, which is the funeral of fame. Oh, the bitterness and misery of renown!"

"Choose yet again," said the fairy. "Two gifts remain. And do not despair. In the beginning, there was but one that was precious, and it is still here."

"I take wealth, which is power! How blind I was!" said the man. "Now, at last, life will be worth the living. I will spend, squander, dazzle. These mockers and despisers will crawl in the dirt before me, and I will feed my hungry heart with their envy. I will have all luxuries, all joys, all enchantments of the spirit, all contentment of the body that man holds dear. I will buy, buy, buy! I have lost much time, and chosen badly heretofore, but I was ignorant then, and now am wiser."

Three short years went by, and a day came when the man sat shivering, gaunt, wan and hollow-eyed, clothed in rags, gnawing a dry crust and mumbling, "Curse all the world's gifts, for mockeries and gilded lies! They are not gifts, but merely lendings. Pleasure, Love, Fame, and Riches are but temporary disguises for the lasting realities of Pain, Grief, Shame, and Poverty. The fairy said true. There was but one gift which was precious, only one that was not valueless. Bring it! I am weary, I would rest."

The fairy came, bringing again four of the gifts, but Death was not among them. She said, "I gave it to a mother's pet, a little child. It was ignorant, but trusted me, asking me to choose for it."

"Although the option was always available to you, you did not ask me to choose. So now, you must simply wait for Death to come."

INTRODUCTION TO

A FABLE

As with *The Five Boons of Life*, this short fable was written by Twain toward the end of his life and was much tighter than many earlier writings. Only minimal editing was necessary for most of the story. On the other hand, Twain develops a wonderful theme here and then leaves it hanging at the end in a way that is strangely unsatisfying. Once again, I have significantly changed the ending to better reflect my view of what the story is really about.

A FABLE

Adapted by Steve Daut,
Twain original first published in 1909

Once upon a time, an artist who had painted a small and very beautiful picture placed it so that he could see it in the mirror. He said, "This doubles the distance and softens it, and it is twice as lovely as it was before." The animals out in the woods heard of this through the housecat, who they greatly admired because he was so learned, so he could tell them many things they didn't know before.

All the animals were excited about this new piece of gossip, and they asked questions in order to get a full understanding of it. They asked what a picture was, for none of them had ever seen one before. The cat explained. "It is a flat thing, wonderfully flat, marvelously flat, enchantingly flat and elegant. And, oh, so beautiful!"

That excited them almost to a frenzy, and they said they would give the world to see it.

The bear asked, "What is it that makes it so beautiful?"

"It's the looks of it," said the cat.

This filled them with admiration and uncertainty, and they were more excited than ever. Then the cow asked, "What is a mirror?"

"It is a hole in the wall," said the cat. "You look in it, and there you see the picture, and it's so dainty and charming and ethereal and inspiring in its unimaginable beauty that your head turns round and round, and you almost swoon with ecstasy."

The donkey had not said anything as yet. He now began to throw doubts. He said there had never been anything so beautiful as to make him swoon with ecstasy, and there probably wasn't now. He said that it was easy to claim something was beautiful, but without more than fancy words about the thing, it was time for suspicion. It was easy to see that these doubts were having an effect upon the animals, so the cat went off offended.

The animals dropped the subject for a couple of days, but curiosity was taking a fresh hold of them, and there was a revival of interest. The animals began to assail the donkey for spoiling what could have been a pleasure to them, merely on his suspicion that the picture was not beautiful, without any evidence that such was the case. The donkey was not troubled. "There's only one way to find out who is right. I will go and look in that hole, then come back and tell what I find there."

The animals felt relieved and grateful, and asked him to go at once. But once he got to the artist's house, he discovered that the artist was not there. He saw the mirror, but he did not know where he ought to stand. So, by mistake, he stood between the picture and the mirror. He moved closer and closer to the mirror until his nose touched it, but all he could see was himself. The picture had no chance, and didn't show up. He returned home and said: "The cat lied. There was nothing in that hole but a donkey. It was a handsome donkey, but just a donkey and nothing more."

The elephant, who was king of all the animals, asked, "Did you see it good and clear? Were you close to it?"

"I saw it good and clear, O Hathi, King of Beasts. I was so close that I touched noses with it."

"This is very strange," said the elephant. "The cat was always truthful before, as far as we could make out. Let another witness try. Go, Baloo, look in the hole, then come and report."

So Baloo, the bear, went. When he came back, he said, "Both the cat and the donkey have lied. There was nothing in the hole but a bear."

Great was the surprise and puzzlement of the animals. Each was now anxious to make the test himself and get at the straight truth. The elephant sent them one at a time. First, the cow, who found nothing but a cow. The tiger found only a tiger, the lion found a lion, and so forth with all of the animals. Finally, the elephant himself went to look and, as with the others, saw only himself in the mirror. He berated all of the other animals for lying, and the jungle became a much less friendly place after that.

Now you know the truth. If you stand between life and the mirror of your imagination, you find only what you bring to it. You may not see what others see, but just because you are right doesn't mean that they are wrong.

THE NOTORIOUS JUMPING FROG OF CALAVERAS COUNTY

As with some other Twain stories, this one went through a fair number of revisions in different publications. In what appears to be the first publication, *Jim Smiley and His Jumping Frog* appeared in the *Saturday Press* on November 18, 1865. It was reprinted in *The Californian* on December 16, 1865, where the story was entitled *The Celebrated Jumping Frog of Calaveras County*, and the main character's name was not Jim Smiley, but Jim Greeley. Greeley became Smiley again after *The Californian* publication, and the frog became notorious by 1872.

In every version I have seen, the story begins with a 400-word introduction that has the narrator looking up a man named Simon Wheeler on behalf of a friend, with the purpose of inquiring about a man named Leonidas W. Smiley (or Greeley), a minister of the Gospel. Wheeler suggests that perhaps the narrator is talking about a feller named Jim Smiley (Greeley), who was around in '49 or '50. This becomes a frame for the actual story of the jumping frog. I'm not sure what the purpose of the frame was, but perhaps, as with many tall tales, it was designed to give the story an air of credibility.

This is a significant revision, highly condensed from the original version, which runs to around 2,500 words. In this version, I have also deviated from the original by placing the action in a bar in town, rather than "an old dilapidated tavern in the ancient mining camp at Angel's."

THE NOTORIOUS JUMPING FROG OF CALAVERAS COUNTY

Adapted by Steve Daut,
Twain original first published in 1865

There was a feller name of Jim Smiley, and he was the bettingest man you ever did see. He'd bet on anything, and if he couldn't get anyone to bet against him, he'd change sides. But for all that, he was uncommon lucky. No matter which side he ended up betting on, he pretty much always came out the winner. After a horse race, he'd be throwing money around every which way. Either that or he was dead broke. He'd bet on a dog fight, a cat fight, or a chicken fight. If there were two birds sitting on a fence, he'd bet you which one would fly first. If there was a cloud on the horizon he'd bet you if it was going to rain or not, how soon and how much. If he saw a straddle-bug going anywhere, he'd bet how long it would take that bug to go wherever it was going, and if you took him up on it, he'd follow that straddle-bug to Mexico just to find out where it was going and how long it took.

He had this friend name of Walker, and Walker's wife got real sick. One day Smiley asked Walker how his sick wife was doing and Walker said, "Well, that poor woman has been mighty sick. I was afraid we was gonna lose her, but she's considerable better lately and I reckon she'll pull through." Well, Smiley couldn't help himself and before he even thought about it, he said, "I'll bet you two dollars that she don't."

Smiley had this old mare, and she was the saddest looking piece of horseflesh you ever wanted to see. She was slow as molasses and always had something wrong, like she was lame or had the consumption, or asthma, or distemper or something like that, and he'd race her. They'd always give her two or three hundred yards head start because they felt sorry for the old nag, and even then she struggled. The field would pass her and she'd wheeze along through the whole race trying to catch up but at the end, she'd get all excited and start kicking up them spindly legs, coughing and blowing her nose and somehow manage to end up a neck ahead, every time.

Well, Smiley had a rat-terrier he called Andrew Jackson, and he had these fighting cocks, and tom-cats and all them kind of things, and if you came up with anything at all, he'd find something to match you. One day he ketched this frog and decided to educate him and so he took him into his back yard and spent three months doing nothing but teaching that frog how to jump. And when he taught something, that critter stayed taught. He'd give that frog a little punch in the rear end and it would spring up in the air, whirling and spinning like a top and would plop down on all fours just like a cat. The way he got him going like this was to point out flies, and that frog could nail a fly in mid-air as far away as the back of the room. He called this frog Daniel Webster, and it got to the place where all Smiley would have to do was say, "Flies! Daniel, flies," and that frog would take to jumping all over the place. Yet that frog was just as humble and pleasant as any frog ever was. But he was gifted, that frog. He won every contest he ever was in, and Smiley was monstrous proud of him.

Well, Smiley kept this frog in a little lattice box, and kept it with him most all the time. One day this stranger came into the bar where Smiley was sitting, and said, "What might you have in the box?"

Smiley acted kind of coy and indifferent and said, "Well, I might have a parrot or a canary, but I don't. It's just a frog."

The man looked in the box and said, "Well, so it is. What's a frog good for, then?"

So Smiley said, "Well, this particular frog is good for one thing. He can out-jump any frog in Calaveras County."

Well, the man said, "I don't see anything about him that makes him so much different than any other frog," and Smiley says, "Well maybe you don't and then again maybe you don't know nothing about frogs. But I got my opinion, and I'll wager forty dollars he can outjump any frog in Calaveras County."

The feller took a good long look in the box, and then a good long look at Smiley and then said, "Well, I'm not from Calaveras County and I got no frog, but if I did, I'd take that wager."

Well, Smiley knew he had him then, and he said, "Look, that's all right. There's a bog pretty close to here. If you hold this box for a minute or two, I'll go out there and catch one for you." So the feller took the box, they each put up their forty dollars, and Smiley went out to catch him a frog. As soon as Smiley was gone, the feller went over to the hardware store across the street, went to the ammunition counter and bought him some quail shot, then he went back to the bar and took a teaspoon and filled that frog up with quail shot – filled him pretty much up to the brim. And when Smiley got back they set them frogs on the floor right down beside each other, and Smiley did a countdown and on the count of three they prodded the frogs from behind and that stranger's frog jumped off real lively, but Daniel just sat there, solid as a church. He hunched up and tried his best but he couldn't push off for all that quail shot inside him.

Well, the feller took the money and started off and when he got to the door, he turned around and kinda smiled and said, "Like I said, I don't see anything about him that makes him so much different than any other frog," and he walked out the door.

Smiley just stood there looking quite perplexed for a spell, and at last he says, "Must be something wrong with Daniel. Best I can figure, he's feeling bad or something. He looks a mite baggy somehow," and he goes to pick him up. When he does his eyes get wide and he says, "Well, blame my cats, if that frog don't weigh five pounds," and he turns him upside down and that frog belches out a double handful of quail shot. Well, Smiley turned red, set that frog down in his box and took out after that stranger ready to tear him apart. But as you can imagine the feller was already long gone.

Well, you woulda thought Smiley would be done with betting after that, but the next time I saw him he was walking this yeller one-eyed cow with three legs. It didn't have no tail, but just a short stump like a banana. I don't know what he was doing with it, but there's no doubt he was working that cow up for a wager of some sort.

THE UNDERTAKER'S CHAT

This story was first published in the October 23, 1870 issue of the *Chicago Tribune* under the title "A Reminiscence of the Back Settlements." In 1882 it appeared in Mark Twain's *Sketches, New and Old* under the current title. The story illustrates some of the burial customs of the time but it also touches on a lot of universal themes that haven't changed in the hundred and fifty years since this story was written. The original is a bit heavy on vernacular, which can be wonderful from the lips of a talented storyteller, but I have toned it down a little bit because a little goes a long way.

This story actually reminded me of a funeral we had in Chelsea when the chief of police and one of the local volunteer firefighters died in a helicopter accident. When they got to the music and played the theme from *Ghostbusters*, a lot of people in the audience were really uncomfortable, as if it was sacrilegious somehow. But it was a request from the firefighter's wife, because it was his favorite song. I thought it was a great touch, because made us think about who, and what, a funeral is for. And it was exactly what my firefighter friend Matt would have wanted.

THE UNDERTAKER'S CHAT

Adapted by Steve Daut,
Twain original first published in 1870

"Now that corpse," said the undertaker, patting the folded hands of the deceased approvingly, "was a brick, every way you took him. He was accommodating, modest, and simple in his last moments. His friends wanted a metallic burial-case, but I couldn't get one and it was clear to see that there warn't going to be time."

"The corpse said never mind, just get him a box he could stretch out in comfort. Said he went more on room than style."

"His friends wanted a silver door-plate on the coffin, signifying who he was and where he was from."

"What did the corpse say? He said whitewash his old canoe and paint his general destination onto it with a brush and a stencil-plate, add a verse from some likely hymn or other, mark him C. O. D., and send him off to the tomb. He warn't distressed any more than you are, but just as calm and collected as a hearse-horse. He said he figured that where he was going he'd rather attract attention by a picturesque moral character than a fancy burial-case."

"I'd druther take care of a fine corpse like him than most of them I've tackled the last seven years. There's some satisfaction in buryin' a man like that. He appreciates what you're doin'. He said his relations meant well, but all them preparations was bound to delay the thing more or less, and he didn't wish to be kept layin' around. You never see such a clear head as what he had."

"Well, the relations wanted a big funeral, but the corpse said he was down on flummery, and didn't want any procession. Fill the hearse full of mourners, he said, and get out a stern line and tow him behind."

"He had me measure him and take a whole raft of directions, then he had the minister stand up behind a long box with a table-cloth over it to represent the coffin and read his funeral sermon. Then he made them trot out the choir so he could help them pick out the tunes for the occasion. He got them to sing 'Pop Goes the Weasel,' because he'd always liked that tune when he was downhearted, and solemn music made him sad. When they sung that with tears in their eyes (because they all loved him), and his relations grieving around, he just laid there as happy as a bug, trying to beat time and showing all over how much he enjoyed it.

"Presently he got worked up and excited, and tried to join in, because he was pretty proud of his abilities in the singing line. But the first time he opened his mouth his breath just took a walk and left him stone cold dead. I never see a man snuffed out so sudden. Ah, it was a great loss to this poor little one-horse town."

"Well, I ain't got time to be chatting any longer. I got to nail on the lid and mosey along with him. If you'll just give me a lift we'll skeet him into the hearse and meander along. His relations like to have it their own way, and most often they don't pay no attention to dying injunctions, the minute a corpse is gone. But if I had my way, I'd tow him behind the hearse just like he asked. Whatever a corpse wants done for his comfort is little enough matter, and a man ain't got no right to deceive him or take advantage of him. Generally, whatever a corpse trusts me to do I'm a-going to do, you know, even if it's to stuff him and paint him yeller and keep him for a keepsake"

The undertaker cracked his whip and went lumbering away with his ancient ruin of a hearse, and I continued my walk, having learned that a healthy and wholesome cheerfulness is not necessarily impossible to any occupation.

EXPERIENCE OF THE MCWILLIAMSES
WITH MEMBRANOUS COUP

This story was first published in 1875. It is the first one of three stories that Twain said were told to him by a "pleasant New York gentleman" named Mr. McWilliams, who he met by accident on a journey. This series of stories was published over a seven-year period.

Indulging in a bit of speculation, I wonder if the mention of McWilliams is Twain's way of paying homage to John McWilliams and his wife Esther, who lived in the same Buffalo boardinghouse as Twain in 1869. Twain became good friends with John and Ester during that time.

EXPERIENCE OF THE MCWILLIAMSES WITH MEMBRANOUS COUP

Adapted by Steve Daut,
Twain original first published in 1875

Back at a time when New York was being ravaged by membranous croup and driving mothers mad with fear, I noted that my wife, Mrs. McWilliams, was allowing our little daughter Penelope to chew on a pine stick.

I said, "You really shouldn't allow that."

"Where's the harm in it, precious?" she replied, although she did take the stick away.

"Love, you should know that pine is the least nutritious wood that a child can eat."

"Hubby, you know better than that. You know you do. All the doctors say that the turpentine in pine wood is good for a weak back and kidneys."

"Sweetheart, I had no idea little Penelope had kidney and spine problems."

"Who said she was having such problems?"

"My love, you just did."

"I never said anything of the kind. And anyway, there isn't any harm in letting her chew a bit of pine stick." At this, she gave the stick back to little Penelope.

"Ah, I see the force of your argument, dearest. I shall go and order three cords of the best pine wood today. No child of mine shall go hungry for a lack of turpentine."

"Stop it right now. Go to your office and leave me in peace." At this, she grabbed the child and bustled off with a flourish.

That evening at dinner, she confronted me with a face white as a sheet. "Another boy in the neighborhood is stricken! Little Georgie Gordon is taken with the membranous croup. There's no hope for him at all. And Penelope played with him last week! I'm sending out for the doctor this very minute."

That evening as our little Penelope was saying her prayers, right in the middle of "Now I lay me down to sleep", she gave a slight cough. My wife fell back as if struck by death itself. She commanded that I move the crib to our room, and she oversaw the process just to make sure I had done it correctly. But once there, my wife said we were too far away from the other baby, and what if he were to have symptoms in the night? So the crib went back into the nursery and we put up a cot for ourselves in the adjoining room. But then, what if the boy should catch the dreaded membranous croup from Penelope? So the crib came out of the nursery again and was installed beside the cot.

Later on that evening, Mrs. McWilliams slipped into the nursery once again and came back with a new dread.

"The baby is sleeping the sleep of the dead. His breathing is so regular. What could make him sleep so soundly?"

"The baby always sleeps like a graven image."

"I know, but somehow this time, there's something frightful about it. Do you think we should call the doctor again?"

"No dearest, I think he'll be just fine. Now come back to bed."

At that moment, Penelope coughed twice in her sleep.

"Where is that doctor? He should be here by now. Mortimer, it's too warm for the poor sick child. Please, turn off the register and check on the doctor."

I got up wearily, preparing to go out into the cold night and track down the doctor, but there was a message on the door from the coachman. The doctor had taken ill and was confined to his bed. But he had sent medicine.

When I took the medicine up to my wife, she cried, "Why would he send medicine when he knows the disease is incurable? He must have sent it just to make us feel better. He's only giving us some hope for a few precious moments. This must mean that the poor thing doesn't stand a chance."

"Why, Dear, perhaps a little might help. It says a tablespoon."

"What do you know about nursing a sick child, Mortimer? Come here, Penelope Dear, here, have a spoonful of this. It'll help you sleep. Put your head on Mother's breast and go to sleep. There there, now. Oh, Mortimer, the poor thing can't live through the night! She needs another tablespoon full. And she needs belladonna, too, I know she does, and aconite! Bring the goose grease as well. Do it, Mortimer, let me do it my way. You know nothing of such things."

I brought the array of remedies she requested and fell immediately back to sleep, exhausted. It was not more than five minutes later that she aroused me again.

"Mortimer, is that register on?"

"No, my love."

"Well, it's freezing in here. Please turn it on at once."

I got up in the dark so as not to wake little Penelope, then turned the durned thing back on again but as I was returning to bed

I had a collision with the rug and woke the child. Stumbling back again, I stepped on the cat, who let out a hideous howl and I automatically kicked out at it, connecting instead with the chair. I let out my own piteous moan and turned on the light to survey the damage to my throbbing metatarsal.

"Now you've done it, Mortimer! Not only have you woken the child, but you've terrorized the cat. And look at that poor chair!"

"But look at my poor foot!"

"Well, you only have yourself to blame. It wouldn't have happened you hadn't tried to kick the poor kitty across the room."

"Can we just drop it and get some sleep?"

Somehow, I managed to get another fifteen minutes of sleep before my wife woke me again.

"Mortimer, it's still freezing in here. I'm trying to give our poor child more medicine and apply some more goose grease, but it's so cold I can't apply it properly."

I got up and started the fire, then sat down disconsolate. Mrs. McWilliams tried to coax me back to bed, but a wood fire is not a permanent thing. I had to renew it every twenty minutes, so I spent the rest of the night sleeping fitfully in the chair and renewing the fire periodically. Every once in a while, the child would cough a bit and Mrs. McWilliams would whirl into a flurry of activity, feeding the poor girl more medicine, re-applying goose grease, adding flax-seed poultices and adding or taking away bedclothes from the child depending on her changing perception of the room temperature.

Finally, I must have passed out from exhaustion, my strength gone and my soul worn out. It was broad daylight when I felt a grip on my shoulder that brought me suddenly to my senses. My wife was glaring down at me and gasping.

"It's all over!" she said. "The child's perspiring! What shall we do?"

"Maybe we should scrape off the goose grease and cool the place down again. It's burning up in here."

"Idiot! There's not a moment to lose! Go get the doctor. Tell him he must come, dead or alive."

I made my way to the doctor's house, dragged the poor sick man out of bed, and brought him to little Penelope's bedside. He took one look at the child and said she was not dying, which seemed to me like it was good news, but it made Mrs. McWilliams as angry as if it was a slap across the face. The doctor said the child's cough was caused by some trifling irritation of the throat. At this he gave her a tincture that sent her into a spasm of coughing and she coughed up a little splinter of wood.

He said, "This is not membranous croup. The child has been chewing on a pine shingle or something and got a sliver in her throat. No harm done."

"No," I said. "I'm sure it hasn't hurt her a bit. In fact, I understand that the turpentine in them is actually good for certain sorts of diseases. My wife will tell you so."

But she didn't tell him anything. She turned and left the room, and we have never referred to the incident again, thus ensuring that our days flow by in deep and untroubled serenity.

INTRODUCTION TO

A GHOST STORY

A Ghost Story was first published in 1875 in a volume entitled *Sketches New and Old*, a collection of stories. The story only works if the audience is familiar with the actual story of the Cardiff Giant, and I have found that it works the best when the complete Cardiff Giant story is told first with no reference to the Twain story. That way, when the giant is revealed in *A Ghost Story*, the audience experiences almost the same impact it would have had in Twain's time. This is not always possible in a storytelling situation, so as an alternative I have added a note in parenthesis where you can add an abbreviated account of the Cardiff Giant story. When I do it that way, I step out of the Twain story for a moment and tell it as a "story within the story". This, of course, is definitely not the preferred way to do it, but it can (sort of) work in a pinch.

As a side note, I have visited P.T. Barnum's giant at Marvin's Marvelous Mechanical Museum in Farmington, Michigan, and not only is the giant worth seeing, but the museum is great fun, as it is chock full of pinball machines, old crank toys, a mechanical one-man band, and all sorts of arcane and wonderful mechanisms. You just have to wonder at things like the mechanical coin-operated Spanish Inquisition.

THE CARDIFF GIANT

A true story,
as told by Steve Daut

The Cardiff Giant is one of the most famous hoaxes in American history. In the 1860's, an atheist tobacconist named George Hull attended a Methodist revival meeting and got into an argument over Genesis 6:4, which states, "There were giants in the Earth in those days." In response, Hull commissioned a German stonecutter to create a ten and a half foot tall giant out of a slab of gypsum. The figure was made to look ancient by treating it with acid and stains, and beating it up with knitting needles. Then it was buried in Cardiff, New York, behind the barn of Hull's cousin, Stub Newell.

About a year later, Newell hired some workers to dig a well in that exact spot, and they were surprised to find what seemed to be a gigantic petrified man. News of the discovery spread, and Newell began charging a steady stream of visitors 50 cents apiece to view the giant. Hull sold his interest in the giant to a syndicate for the sum of $23,000, a sum equivalent to over $400,000 today. The syndicate moved the giant to Syracuse, New York for exhibition, and it drew such fantastic crowds that P.T. Barnum offered to lease it for three months for a sum equivalent to at least $1 million today. The syndicate assumed he was going to copy it, so refused to let Barnum have the giant. Not to be deterred, Barnum hired a man to secretly make an exact plaster replica of the creature.

Barnum billed his plaster copy as the real giant, and claimed that the original Cardiff Giant was a fake. Barnum's giant became much more famous than the original, and of course, made a lot more money. In response to Barnum's claim, the head of the syndicate, a man named David Hannum, was quoted in the papers as saying, "There's a sucker born every minute." Ironically, not only did Barnum convince people that his giant was the real fake, but his most famous quote was actually said by the man he stole the giant from.

Barnum also offered the sum of $1,000 to anyone who could prove that his giant was less authentic than the syndicate's. The syndicate sued Barnum for calling their giant a fake, since theirs was the original. Apparently, the judge responded with a statement to the effect that if the giant was real, it should speak for itself. At any rate, the court ruled that Barnum couldn't be sued for calling a fake giant a fake, even if it was the original fake.

The original Cardiff Giant apparently wound up in a farmer's basement as a coffee table until it was sold to the Farmer's Museum in Cooperstown, New York in 1947, where it continues to be displayed. The copy created by P.T. Barnum is currently at Marvin's Marvelous Mechanical Museum in Farmington Hills, Michigan. A third replica, created in 1972, is on display at the Fort Museum & Frontier Village at Fort Dodge, Iowa, acknowledging the area where the original stone was cut and the hoax was born.

A GHOST STORY

Adapted by Steve Daut,
Twain original first published in 1875

When I took the room in a huge old largely abandoned building, way up in Broadway, for the first time in my life I experienced a dark and superstitious dread. As I turned the dark angle of the stairway and an invisible cobweb clung to my face, I shuddered as if I had encountered a phantom.

Finally, I reached my room and locked out the mold and the darkness. The warm fire burning in the grate gave me a sense of relief, and I sat for hours recalling old times and listening to imagined voices and songs from long ago. Slowly, my thoughts grew progressively sadder as the rain against the windows diminished to a steady patter and the shrieking wind diminished to a wail. A sense of profound loneliness crept over me and I covered up in bed, listening to the rain, winds, and creaking shutters until they lulled me to sleep.

I don't know how long I slept, but I awoke to the fevered beating of my own heart. As the darkened world began to coalesce around me, I felt the bedclothes begin to slip slowly toward to foot of the bed, as if some unseen hand were pulling them.

They continued slipping until my chest was uncovered, and with a great effort I grabbed at them and pulled them above my head. I waited and listened, and the blankets began slipping once again. Grabbing on more tightly, I again pulled them up but the steady tug from below increased, until I grunted with the strain of struggle. An answering groan came from the foot of the bed. As the beads of sweat rose on my forehead, I heard the footsteps of something huge and heavy moving away from me, then through the closed door and out of the room, leaving me in a silence filled with dread.

"This is just a dream, a hideous dream," I told myself, and just to confirm my desperate assurances, I arose and checked the doors. They were bolted and locked, just as I had left them. I lit a pipe and sat down by the fire, and what I saw there in the ashes on the hearth caused the pipe to fall from my nerveless fingers and the blood to drain from my face. There, beside my footprint in the ashes was another print, a print so enormous that it made mine look like that of a child. I did have a visitor, one of elephantine proportions!

I went back to bed, seeking the solace of sleep until the morning came, but the night swirled around me, with grating noises overhead, the slamming of doors in distant parts of the building, half-uttered screams cut off midway through, the rush of invisible wings. I felt warm gouts of blood splatter my body, saw luminous faces floating above me, whispering dread imaginings into my fevered brain. Once again, I rose to sit by the fire, contemplating the meaning of the massive footprint in the ashes of the hearth. As I sat, the elephantine tread began again, this time moving into the room and toward me. There was a huge, cloudy presence moving toward me in the flickering gloom of the firelight. Gradually, the figure took shape – an arm, then a body, and finally a great sad face looked out of the vapor. Naked, muscular and comely, the majestic Cardiff Giant loomed above me.

(NOTE: If I have not told an audience the Cardiff Giant story before this, it is here that I insert an abbreviated account of that story. I simply indicate that I am stepping out of the Twain story for a moment to give a brief account of the Giant as one of the most famous hoaxes in American history.)

On seeing the giant, all my mystery vanished, for even a child knows that this friendly giant would mean no harm. So I greeted him warmly.

"Well, I'm glad to see it is only you. I have been scared to death for the last three hours. I wish I had a chair that could contain you. Wait! No! Don't sit there!"

I was too late. The chair was demolished. But the giant could not be contained. Three chairs later, he still would not listen.

"Confound it, have you no judgment at all? Will you ruin all of the furniture in the house, you petrified fool?"

Apparently, he was bent on doing just that. He moved from

the chairs to the bed, which was soon a melancholy ruin.

"What way is that to treat a welcoming host? You come lumbering in here bringing a legion of vagabond goblins, worrying me to death, and even though I ignore the fact that you are completely naked, you begin wrecking all of the furniture in the place, and you damage yourself in the process. Look at you! You have broken off a piece of your spinal column and chipped up your hams until the place looks like a marble yard."

"Well, I am truly sorry about the furniture, but what can I do? I have not had a chance to sit down for a century." And with that, he began to cry.

"Poor devil. I didn't mean to be so harsh. Please have a seat on the floor, over here by the fire."

He sat, and I brought him a pipe to smoke, my red blanket to wrap himself in and my washbasin for a hat. After we spoke for an hour, I noticed that he looked tired, and I commented on it.

"Well, of course I'm tired. I'm the ghost of the Cardiff Giant who resides at the museum across the street. Oh, how I wish I were back behind old Newell's barn. It was restful there. I will have no rest until they bury the poor body again, but instead they display it for all to see, all day long. I tried haunting the place, to try and get them to return the body to its resting place, but no one comes to the museum at night. So I thought

I would come over here and try haunting this place a little, trying to rouse someone to my cause. Do you know how tiring it is to drag chains around, groan, whisper, and tramp up and down chairs? Can't you give me any hope at all?"

I jumped to me feet. "Why you poor blundering old fossil! You're haunting the wrong body! That display across the street is but a plaster cast of the body. The real Cardiff Giant is in Albany. Confound it man, don't you know your own body?"

I have never seen a more pitiable humiliation in my life. The ghost rose to his feet, set down my pipe on the mantel, and said, "Honestly, is that true?"

"As true as I'm sitting here."

"Well, I've never felt so absurd. The Petrified Man sold everything else, and now the scoundrel has sold his own ghost! If you have any charity in your heart, don't let this out to anyone. Think of how you would feel if you had made such an ass of yourself."

At that, he turned slowly and tramped down the stairs into the deserted street. I was sorry that he had gone, poor fellow, but sorrier still that he had carried away my red blanket and washbasin.

INTRODUCTION TO

THE SALESMAN'S TALE

This story was originally called *The Canvasser's Tale*. A canvasser is someone who goes door-to-door soliciting information or opinions, or trying to sell something. In the case of this story, it refers to a door-to-door salesman, but even that is an anachronism today. I thought briefly about bringing this tale more fully into the current times by creating some sort of online store but part of Twain's appeal is the cordial humanity of his stories and I couldn't bring myself to remove it that far from human interaction. Perhaps that is an exercise for future generations as interactions, I fear, may become more and more impersonal. I hope I'm wrong on that score.

As with some other stories in this collection, I have rearranged the story somewhat in order to make it flow better for the storyteller. Structurally, the original has a few continuity issues that can pull people out in the telling and these, also, have been addressed.

THE SALESMAN'S TALE

Adapted by Steve Daut,
Twain original first published in 1876

Poor, sad-eyed stranger! There was something about his humble manner, his tired look, his expensive but frayed clothes, which spoke to the charity that still remained, remote and lonely, in the empty vastness of my heart. I observed a portfolio under his arm, and knew that Providence had delivered me into the hands of yet another salesman. Still, he had my sympathy, so I let him in. His story went something like this:

"My parents died when I was but a little child. My uncle reared me as his own. He was my only relative in the wide world, but he was good and rich and generous. He reared me in the lap of luxury, and I had everything money could satisfy. After I graduated, I went with two of my servants to travel in foreign countries. In those far lands I reveled in the riches I discovered, but of all things, what appealed to me the most was the prevailing custom among the rich, that of collecting elegant and costly rarities. I wrote and told my uncle of one gentleman's vast collection of shells, another's noble collection of meerschaum pipes, another's priceless collection of old china, and so forth."

"Soon my letters yielded fruit. My uncle began to look about for something to collect. Although I was not aware of it, his frenzy to create a collection soon became a raging fever. He began to neglect his great pork business. Soon he sold the business, retired and turned an elegant leisure into a rabid search for curious things. He did not spare his vast wealth on this new obsession. First, he tried cow-bells. He made a collection that filled five large rooms and comprised all the different sorts of cow-bells that ever had been contrived, except one. That one, an antique, and the only specimen left, was possessed by another collector. My uncle offered enormous sums for it, but the gentleman would not sell. A true collector attaches no value to a collection that's not complete, so my uncle's great heart broke and he sold the entire collection for next to nothing."

"He turned his mind to finding some field that seemed unoccupied. He tried brickbats, then flint hatchets and other implements of Primeval Man, then Aztec inscriptions and stuffed whales, but it always turned out the same. After incredible labor and expense, he would get to the final item to complete each collection and insurmountable obstacles would arise. He knew another disappointment might kill him, but finally resolved with what was left of his resources, to select one final passion that no one else was collecting. He carefully made up his mind, and decided to make a collection of echoes."

"Now you may know that in the echo market the scale of prices is cumulative, like the carat-scale in diamonds. An echo that repeats only once, also known as a single-carat echo, is worth but ten dollars over and above the value of the land it is on. A two-carat or double-barreled echo is worth thirty dollars, a five-carat is worth nine hundred and fifty, and a ten-carat is worth thirteen thousand, plus the value of the land. And it goes up from there."

"My uncle's first purchase was an echo in Georgia that repeated four times, his next was a six-repeater in Maryland, and his next was a twelve-repeater in Tennessee, which he got cheap because it was out of repair. A portion of the crag which reflected it had tumbled down. He believed he could repair it at a cost of a few thousand dollars, and, by increasing the elevation with masonry, triple the repeating capacity. But the architect who undertook the job had never built an echo before, and so he utterly spoiled this one. It used to talk back like a mother-in-law, but after he meddled with it, the thing never spoke without permission."

"Next he bought a lot of cheap little double-barreled echoes scattered around over various states, which he got at twenty percent off by taking the entire lot. Then he bought a machine gun of an echo in Oregon, and it cost a fortune, I can tell you. My uncle's Oregon-echo, which he called the Great Pitt Echo, was a twenty-two-carat gem, and cost two hundred and sixteen thousand dollars on top of the cost of the land itself."

"Then that divine echo, known throughout the world as the Great Koh-i-noor, or Mountain of Repetitions, was discovered. It was a sixty-five-carat gem. You could utter a single word and it would talk back at you for fifteen minutes. The property consisted of a couple of small hills with a shallow swale in between, out yonder among the back settlements of New York State. But another echo-collector was in the field. My uncle and the other collector arrived on the ground at the same time, and neither knew the other was there. Williamson Bolivar Jarvis owned the east hill, and Harbison J. Bledso owned the west hill. The swale between was the dividing line. So while my uncle was buying Jarvis's hill for three million two hundred and eighty-five thousand dollars, the other collector was buying Bledso's hill for a shade over three million."

"The natural result was that the noblest collection of echoes on earth was forever and ever incomplete, since it possessed but one-half of the king echo of the universe. Neither man was content with this divided ownership, yet neither would sell to the other. There were jawings, bickerings, heart-burnings. At last that other collector, with a malignancy that only a collector can ever feel toward a man and a brother, announced that if he couldn't have the echo, then no one should have it. He'd remove his hill, and then there would be nothing to reflect my uncle's echo."

"Well, my uncle got an injunction to stop this man from destroying the hill. They fought their battle all the way up to the Supreme Court of the United States. It was finally decided that the two men were separate and independent owners of the two hills, but tenants in common in the echo. Therefore, the defendant was at full liberty to cut down his hill, since it belonged solely to him, but if he did he would have to pay my uncle three million dollars as damages to my uncle's half of the echo. The decision debarred my uncle from using the defendant's hill to reflect his part of the echo without the defendant's consent. The court also debarred the defendant from using my uncle's hill to reflect his end of the echo, without consent. Neither man would give consent, so that astonishing and most noble echo had to cease from its great powers. Though the magnificent property is still intact, it is tied up and unsalable."

"Then came news of my uncle's death, and also a copy of his will, making me his sole heir. I was heir to a vast collection of echoes. But I was also head and ears in debt. There was not an echo in the lot without a mortgage on it."

"Now, sir, if you will be so kind as to look at these maps and plans in my portfolio, I'm sure I can sell you an echo for less money than any man in the trade. This one for instance, which cost my uncle ten thousand dollars thirty years ago, is one of the sweetest things in Texas. But I'll let you have it for—"

"Stop," I said. "My friend, although I have let you go on with your story, I have not had a moment's respite from salesmen this day. I bought a sewing machine that I didn't want, a map that's mistaken in all its details, a clock that does not go. I've bought no end of useless inventions, and now I've had enough of this foolishness. I wouldn't have one of your echoes if you were even to give it to me. Take your collection and move on."

INTRODUCTION TO

MRS MCWILLIAMS AND THE LIGHTNING

This is the second installment of the McWilliams series. Once again, Twain framed it as a conversation with Mr. McWilliams, and once again it seems to me that the frame distracts from the story, so I eliminated it. In this case, I took some information from the frame at the end and moved it up into the story. The abrupt ending I offer here is designed to have more audience impact than the original, as Twain's sequence seems anti-climactic.

MRS MCWILLIAMS AND THE LIGHTNING

Adapted by Steve Daut,
Twain original first published in 1880

It was my experience that mainly dogs had a deathly fear of lightning, until I married my wife, that is. She was otherwise a strong and bold woman. She could face a mouse, a spider, or the devil himself without batting an eye, but her unreasoning fear of lightning was pitiful to see.

One night I awoke to her cries wailing in my ears, "Mortimer! Mortimer!"

"Where are you, Evangeline?" I said, for she was nowhere to be seen.

"Here in the closet. You should be ashamed of yourself, sleeping like that with such a horrible storm going on."

"But dear," I said, "it's unreasonable for you to expect me to be ashamed while I'm asleep. Give me a moment to wake up so I can become properly ashamed."

Just then a terrible boom and flash of light occurred, and I heard a gasp and muffled sobs from the closet. "I'm sorry," I said. "I didn't mean to make light of your predicament."

"Then come out of that bed instantly. Have you no care for me or the children? You know there is no place so dangerous as a bed in such a thunderstorm."

"But I'm up and out of bed, trying to find the candle."

"Don't light a match! Are you stark raving mad?"

"But I can't see anything," I said as I struck the match.

"Put it out immediately! You know that nothing attracts lightning like a light!" As if to underscore her comment, a series of loud crashes, booms, and fizzles pierced the air. "Now see what you've done!"

"No, I don't see what I've done. A light might attract lighting, I don't know, but I do know it doesn't cause it. And if those shots were aimed at my match, it was blessed poor marksmanship."

"For shame, Mortimer! Here we are in the very presence of death and you use such language as that. Did you say your prayers tonight? Because if not—"

Crash! Boom!

"Oh, we're surely lost beyond all help! How could you neglect to say your prayers at a time like this?"

"But Dear, the times were not like this when we went to bed. There wasn't a cloud in the sky. How was I to know that there would be all this rumpus and powwow about a little slip like that? I haven't missed saying my prayers since I brought on the earthquake four years ago."

"Mortimer! How can you say that? Have you forgotten about the yellow fever?"

"Evangeline, you are always throwing up the yellow fever to me, and that's perfectly unreasonable. My devotional slip that evening could never reach as far as Memphis. I'll accept the earthquake because it was local, but I'll be hanged if I'm going to accept responsibility for every—"

B-b-boom! Bang! Crash!

"Mortimer, you aren't standing in front of the fireplace, are you?"

"Yes, Dear, that's the very crime I am committing."

"Don't you know there's no better conductor of lightning than an open chimney?"

At this, I moved away from the chimney and began singing to myself in order to calm my nerves.

"Mortimer, if I told you once, I told you a hundred times, singing causes vibrations in the atmosphere, which interrupt the flow of magnetic vibrations. What on earth are you opening that door for?"

"Goodness gracious, woman, is there any harm in that?"

"Harm? There's *Death* in that. Hurry and shut it, or we're all destroyed!"

I closed it just as another flash and boom rang out.

"Mortimer, did you order the feather bed as I asked you to?"

"Not yet. Why are you thinking about that during such a treacherous time as this?"

"If you had a featherbed now, you could spread it out on the middle of the floor and lie on it, and you'd be perfectly safe. Why don't you just join me in the closet here?"

Well, I tried, but the closet was nowhere big enough for both of us. But I brought her the candle, which she explained would be safe enough if it was in the closet. And I bought her a German book which purported to be a scientific treatise on the nature of lightning.

"It says here," she shouted from the closet, "That the safest place for you is to stand on a chair in the middle of the room, with all four legs in glass tumblers for insulation."

I set up the chair with glasses from the kitchen.

"I'm having a little trouble with my German, Mortimer. Does *einweg* mean away or around?"

"Around, I think."

"OK. Then you are supposed to put something metal around you. Put on your fireman's helmet, buckle on your military saber and get up on the chair."

I did as she commanded just as another flash split the air.

"Oh, wait!" she said, "It also says something about ringing the church bells. Go grab the dinner bell and keep it ringing."

Once again, I did as she said. After I stood on the chair, arrayed with metal and ringing the bell for seven or eight minutes, a lantern was thrust in through the open window and a number of men's heads filled the window space.

"What in the nation is the matter here?" asked my neighbor.

"There's nothing the matter, my friends. Just a little discomfort on account of the thunderstorm. I was trying to keep off the lightning."

"Have you lost your mind? It's a beautiful starlit night, for the Fourth of July. Did you think to look out the window and watch the fireworks?"

One after another of those watching lay down on the ground to laugh. And they laughed real hard. Two of them died.

INTRODUCTION TO

MRS MCWILLIAMS AND THE BURGLAR ALARM

This is the third and final installment in the McWilliams saga. As with the others, I have removed the frame, instead telling it as Mr. McWilliams. The last part is highly condensed from Twain's original, and the whole story has been significantly rearranged in order to make it flow for the storyteller. I have also added my own ending.

MRS MCWILLIAMS AND THE BURGLAR ALARM

Adapted by Steve Daut,
Twain original first published in 1882

Mrs. McWilliams and I had a little money left over from building our house, so we decided to install a burglar alarm. The man came up from New York and put in the alarm, and charged three hundred and twenty-five dollars for it, and said we could sleep easy now, knowing we were protected. We did sleep easy for a month.

Then one night we smelled smoke, so I started toward the stairs and met a burglar coming out of a room with a bag full of tinware, which he must have mistaken for solid silver in the dark. He was smoking a pipe.

I said, "My friend, we do not allow smoking in that room."

He said, "But I'm a stranger, so you could not possibly expect me to know the rules of the house. I've been in many houses just as good as this one, no one objected to it before. And besides, such rules don't apply to burglars, anyway."

I said, "Smoke along, then. But I have to ask what business you have coming into this house without ringing the burglar alarm?"

He looked confused and ashamed, and said, with embarrassment, "I'm terribly sorry. I didn't know you had a burglar alarm, or else I would have rung it. May I trouble you for a match?"

I said, "I don't carry matches in my pajamas. But to return to business, how did you get in here?"

"Through a second-story window."

After some negotiation, I bought back the tinware at pawnbroker's rates and bade the burglar good-night. The next morning I sent for the burglar-alarm man, and he explained that the alarm didn't 'go off' because only the first floor was attached to the alarm. This was simply idiotic. It was like a warrior going into battle with armor only on his legs. The expert put the whole second story on the alarm, charged another three hundred dollars for it, and went his way.

Somewhat later, I found a burglar in the third story, about to start down a ladder with a lot of miscellaneous property. I redeemed the property at bargain rates, after deducting ten percent for the use of my ladder. The next day the expert attached the third story to the alarm, for another three hundred dollars.

By this time the control panel had grown huge, with forty-seven tags on it, marked with the names of the various rooms and chimneys, and it occupied the space of an oversized wardrobe. He added a gong the size of a wash-bowl, and installed it above the head of our bed. We should have been comfortable now but there was one problem. Every morning at five the cook opened the kitchen door, and that gong went off! The first time this happened I thought the Last Days had come. The effect of that frightful gong was to hurl us across the room, slam us into the wall, and curl us up like spiders on a hot stove. We stayed like that until finally, somebody shut the kitchen door. That alarm didn't just wake us in spots, it woke us to the depths of our souls. We were so awake that we didn't even blink for the next eighteen hours.

One night we had a sick friend over for dinner, and he died, right there in the middle of the mashed potatoes. Since it was late, we decided to leave him in our room overnight and call the funeral parlor in the morning. When that terrible gong went off at five the next morning, he jumped up and slammed against the wall, fully revived. He collected his life-insurance and lived happily ever after.

We disconnected that kitchen door for awhile, but the alarm kept going off. Soon the alarm invented a new kink. One winter's night we were flung out of bed by the sudden music of that awful gong, and when we hobbled to the controller and saw the word "Nursery," Mrs. McWilliams fainted dead away. I seized my shotgun and charged into the room, only to find that there was not a sign of a burglar, and no window had been raised. I did in my excitement, however, blast a hole in the window and messed up all the alarm wires and so forth. The alarm expert answered the usual call the next day, and explained that it was a "false alarm." He said it was easily fixed. So he overhauled the nursery window, charged an outrageous price for it, and left.

We suffered from false alarms for the next three years. At first, I always flew in with my gun to the room indicated, but there was never anything to shoot at. We always sent down for the expert the next day, and he fixed those particular windows so they would keep quiet a week or so, and he always remembered to send us a sizeable bill. After we had answered three or four hundred false alarms, we stopped answering them. I simply rose up calmly when slammed into the wall by the gong, inspected the controller, took note of the room indicated and disconnected that room from the alarm. Then I'd go back to bed as if nothing had happened. I'd leave that room off permanently, and wouldn't send for the expert. Over the course of time, all the rooms were taken off, and the entire machine was out of service.

That's when the burglars carried off the burglar alarm! Every hide and hair of it - ripped it out, tooth and nail - springs, bells, gongs, battery, and all. They took a hundred and fifty miles of copper wire. They just cleaned her out, bag and baggage, and never left us a vestige of her to swear at.

The alarm man told us that the system was obsolete by now anyway. What we really needed was the new system that had new springs for the windows that made false alarms impossible and this new patented clock that turned the alarm on and off with no need for human interference. They installed it at a prodigious cost, and all it did was to increase the complicated series of disturbances to our sleep patterns. We tried various options over the next months, installing switches and breakers that mostly didn't work or we forgot to use, and then we found out that a band of burglars had been lodging in the house the whole time. As it turns out, the alarm on our house had gained us the reputation of being the safest place in America. So the police felt no need to monitor it and it became the perfect haven for burglars. For months we couldn't have any company. Not a spare bed in the house. They were all occupied by burglars.

Well, at that point I had slept for years with burglars, maintained an expensive burglar alarm the whole time, for their protection, not mine, and at my sole cost. Yet I couldn't get those burglars to contribute even a dime for the cause. I had come to believe that burglar alarms are made for the benefit of burglars, and definitely not for those who just want a good night's sleep.

The final reckoning came after we experienced an especially terrible series of late night alarms and found that there were no burglars left in the house to help us resolve the problems. Once again, we had to call in the alarm company. A couple of the burglars showed up at the door in brand new company uniforms and explained that they decided to go straight and had purchased the company with the proceeds from the things they had liberated from us. Considering the situation, they offered to make the necessary repairs at discount rates, but I declined. Mrs. McWilliams and I finally had enough, so with her full consent I removed every bit of burglar alarm gadgetry from the house and traded it off for a guard dog.

INTRODUCTION TO

THE THIRTY THOUSAND DOLLAR BEQUEST

This story was originally published in 1904 in a collection of Twain's work by the name, *The $30,000 Bequest and Other Stories*, which mainly included stories first published earlier. The original runs to around 12,000 words, and is divided into 8 chapters, or sections. I found the plotline rather confused in the original, so I had to do quite a bit of re-arranging in order to keep the sequence of events straight in the telling.

Twain uses a somewhat confusing device in this story, giving the characters pet names that flip their sexes – Saladin becomes Sally, and Electra becomes Aleck. Although I'm not quite sure of the reason for this device, I could speculate that Twain found Sally's impulsiveness to be a feminine quality and Aleck's financial acumen to be a male quality, but speculation like that would probably get me in trouble, so I won't indulge. At any rate, I have left the gender confusion in with one difference –I find the hard closing sound of the name "Aleck" seems to slow down the narrative for me, so I change Electra's pet name to Lex, which, for me, flows better in the telling. Still, I have found the gender confusion to be, well, confusing, and I have also had some audience members tell me the same thing, so you might find that it works better to give them pet names that don't introduce this sexual flip.

THE THIRTY THOUSAND DOLLAR BEQUEST

Adapted by Steve Daut,
Twain original first published in 1904

Lakeside was a pleasant little town in the Southwest, where everyone was religious in a good way, and everybody knew everybody and his dog. Saladin Foster, also known as Sally, worked at the general store and at eight hundred dollars a year was the highest paid bookkeeper in Lakeside. But his wife Electra, who he called Lex, had the business sense in the family, She had bought a piece of property for $25 when she was nineteen, and through her financial skills and disciplined savings program, by the time she was thirty-four the couple had built a two thousand dollar house on it, they were out of debt and had a fairly comfortable sum of money in investments, despite a couple of daughters. During the day, both Sally and Lex were thoughtful and calculating but at night they put the plodding world away and read each other fantasy stories, dreaming of kings and princes, of stately lords and ladies in noble palaces and ancient castles.

Then came great news. Tilbury Foster, a vague and indefinite relative of Sally's—an uncle, or perhaps a second or third cousin—sent Sally a letter declaring that he was about to die and would be leaving Sally thirty thousand dollars, not out of familial love but because money had been a pox on his life and he wanted to place it where it would continue to do its malignant work. The bequest would be in his will, but only provided that Sally would never, under any circumstances, reveal the nature or amount of the gift, would not make inquiries regarding Tilbury's death, and would not attend the funeral. As soon as they recovered from the shock, Sally and Lex made a solemn compact to follow these instructions to the letter, and vowed they would never presume to be disobediently thankful for the bequest.

First thing the next morning, Sally subscribed to the Weekly Sagamore so as not to miss the big announcement when it came. Tilbury's letter had come too late for the week's deadline. They would have to wait an entire week to hear of his untimely passing, when and if it happened.

In the meantime, both began dreaming, with visions of thirty thousand sugar plum fairies dancing through their heads. They couldn't focus on their work. All day long, Sally was planning how to spend the money and Lex was planning how to invest it. Each was frantically pursuing their own paper dreams, and by evening each was so invested in their personal future life that they had become silent and distraught.

It was Sally who first broke the silence.

"It will be so grand, Lex! We'll have a horse and buggy for summer, with a bearskin lap blanket for winter..."

"Not out of the principal, dear. Not even if it was a million!"

"But dear, we've worked so long, scrimped and saved. Now that we're rich, it does seem like we could…"

"If we just wait a single year, we could get in on the ground floor with the new coal mines. They'll pay ten percent, and in a year the stock will grow to ninety thousand. I just read about it in the Cincinnati newspaper."

"Ninety thousand! Let's buy it right now!"

"Don't lose your head, dear. We should wait until we actually get the money."

When the paper finally thudded at the door, they tore at the wrapper and scanned the death notices. But Tilbury had disappointed them.

"Damn his treacherous hide!" said Sally.

"How can you say such an evil thing? We can hardly fault the man for staying alive a bit longer. Have a little patience."

"But he's the one who wants to give away the money in order to harm us. I'm just hoping he gets his wish as soon as possible. That's all, dear."

"There's no hurry. I'm sure I can find some other suitable

investments. And when we do start making money I'm sure we can find a little room to get that horse and buggy."

And in fact that very evening, Lex found a way to double their investment to $180,000.

So they waited. Each week, they eagerly scanned the paper for the notice, but Tilbury stubbornly refused to appear, and they became more and more resentful of his delays. They didn't know that they had been wronging the man all along. Tilbury had kept the faith after all, and died to schedule. He was perfectly and completely dead by the time the second weekly issue had come out, but the Weekly Sagamore was a poor little village rag and just as the editorial page was being locked up, Hostetter's Ladies and Gents Ice Cream Parlor had delivered a free quart of strawberry ice cream and Tilbury's announcement got crowded out to make room for the editor's frantic gratitude. And by the next issue, the obituary was long forgotten for more lively matters, so Tilbury's death was never resurrected.

Five weeks drifted along with no mention of Tilbury in the *Weekly Sagamore*. Then six months.

Finally, Sally snapped. "Damn his livers! He's immortal!"

"Don't be impatient," said Lex. "Our assets are piling up by the tens of thousands. We are beginning to roll in eventual wealth, so be grateful for what we're about to have."

But their castle-building habit grew, taking on dimensions they'd never dreamed of before. Lex began to buy fantasy securities on margin in order to increase their financial leverage. Sally began converting their small wood house into a make-believe two-story brick Tudor.

As their imaginary assets grew, so did the real world assets of their two teenage daughters, Gwendolyn and Clytemnestra. Some of the local young men were beginning to take an interest in one sister or another, but with the family's rapidly changing financial status, the girls would need to aim higher. Sally and Lex surveyed the market in order to dangle a higher quality of goods in front of the girls. There was definitely a good crop of rising young doctors and lawyers available, who could be invited to a strategically timed dinner.

But then Lex's late night scheme came to fruition, and their imaginary wealth swelled to well over four hundred thousand. Soon, the doctors and lawyers seemed too lowly, and they began to look for bankers and heirs to local industry. Yet luck came their way again and Lex doubled their accounts to a cold million and the prospect for the girls became the Governor's son and the son of the Congressman.

The Foster fictitious finances grew in leaps and bounds. Everything Lex touched turned into fairy gold, and their wealth increased, seemingly without end. Five million, then ten, then it doubled again and again, to twenty-four hundred million, for an income yield of $120 million per year without ever touching the principal!

"Lex, I have been thinking about this marriage business, and it has been entirely unsatisfying. After the congressman, we considered the son of the Vice President, and then we turned to Europe, considered a few barons, some viscounts and dukes, and though each has proven to be sound in limb and pedigree, they're all bankrupt and in debt up to their ears. We can't afford to bankroll these dandies."

"Sally, what would you say to royalty?"

This revelation knocked Sally dizzy. Of course! It would be the perfect compact between America and the European nations. They then fell silent and drifted away on their dream wings to plan the most grandiose weddings between their two daughters and crowned heads throughout the entire world.

Along with their new international life, their imaginary wealth grew beyond their ability to spend. They were loathe to forgo the weekends on their yacht or their estate in the south of France. The couple drifted in the clouds for days, their heads filled with the rarified air of the upper financial atmosphere. They were so focused on their fantasy worlds that their real-life world began to suffer. Sally sold molasses by the weight, sugar by the yard, and furnished soap when asked for candles. Lex put the cat in the wash and fed milk to the dirty linen.

As they worked nights to keep up with their vast holdings, it began to stretch their mundane real-life finances to the breaking point with all of the candles they were burning. The utility cost of their air mansions grew to dwarf the actual payment on the little wooden house.

Sally had taken to robbing candles from the store where he worked, his morals sullied by the prospect of great wealth. At night he hung out with the moneyed wastrels, multimillionaires in money and paupers in character. He began getting drunk three times a day and breaking the bank at Monte Carlo during his evenings.

Lex became involved in many charitable activities, and it was a cold day when she couldn't ship a cargo of missionaries to persuade Chinamen to trade their twenty-four carat Confucianism for counterfeit Christianity. She began overindulging her financial fantasies. She went into business again, risking their entire fortune to acquire the whole infrastructure of the United States, purchased on margin. The new investment started booming, so she told Sally about it. He was ecstatic. But he was also appalled at the risk she was taking.

"Sell now! We own the whole earth! Want more can we possibly want?"

"Just another few days, dear. My brokers assure me there's another five percent in it."

It was a fatal resolve. The very next day came the historic crash. They were wiped out, and Lex's imaginary brokers had disappeared, much like real-world brokers do when the market drops. Although Sally almost reminded her that he had told her to sell, he held his tongue, realizing that Lex was a broken woman, riddled by regret from her action.

They had only begun to adjust to their newly-paupered life when they were interrupted by the editor and proprietor of the Weekly Sagamore. He was in town for business, and decided to stop by the Fosters house to try and collect the six dollars they owed him from abandoning their subscription four years back. Describing his need for the money, he said, "As they say, money is as tight as Tilbury Foster." When both of them jumped, he realized his error and said, "Oh, I'm sorry. It's just an expression we use. Was he a relative of yours?"

Lex said, "Uh - not that we know of, but is he doing well?"

"Well?", the editor said. "He's been in the ground these past five years!"

Secretly thrilled, Sally tried to put a sad face on it and said, "Well, that's life. Not even the rich are spared the agony of death."

The editor laughed. "Well, that certainly didn't apply to Tilbury. He didn't even have enough to pay for his newspapers. The whole town had to chip in to bury him."

The Fosters paid the six dollars, shooed the editor out the door, and sat in stunned silence. They lived this way for the next two years, and both succumbed on the same day to the call of the next world. Sally's final thoughts were a curse upon Tilbury. "Money had brought him misery," he thought, "and he took his revenge on us, who had done him no harm. What base calculation led him to thirty thousand since a vast fortune would have cost him no more than the amount he gave us, and the thirty ruined our life and broke our hearts. A kinder soul would have made us owners of the world, but he was no generous spirit."

And thus, Sally died.

INTRODUCTION TO

EXCERPT FROM
CAPTAIN STORMFIELD'S VISIT TO HEAVEN

This story apparently was written as early as 1868, but first appeared in print in *Harper's Magazine* in two sections, the first in December 1907 and the second in January 1908. Twain claimed that the early version was a satire of *The Gates Ajar*, by Elizabeth Stuart Ward, which sold briskly in the years following the Civil War. Considered inspirational fiction, Ward's book took its vision of Heaven seriously, and a review of the book claimed it incorporates sermon, diary, sentimental domestic plot, and allegory. A somewhat revised version of Twain's story was later published in book form in 1909. It was the last story published by Mark Twain during his life, and structurally, it is one of Twain's most complex short stories. Since it points out the absurdities of many of people's beliefs about the afterlife as well as the impossibility of finding a perfect situation or physical age in which to spend all of eternity, it is actually a poignant statement of his thoughts during the latter part of his life.

One piece of historical trivia that underscores the strategic timing of this story is that Twain was born in 1835, just two weeks after the orbit of Halley's Comet was closest to the

Sun. The next projected appearance was 1910. According to the Smithsonian Library, Twain was quoted as saying in 1909, "I came in with Halley's comet in 1835. It is coming again next year, and I expect to go out with it. It will be the greatest disappointment of my life if I don't go out with Halley's Comet. The Almighty has said, no doubt: 'Now here are these two unaccountable freaks; they came in together, they must go out together.'" And indeed, he was not disappointed. He died of a heart attack the next year, in 1910. It's certainly no coincidence that Captain Stormfield starts his journey by racing with comets.

A second piece of trivia has to do with the story's name. In 1908, the same year he wrote and published this story, Twain moved into his final home, located in Redding, Connecticut. The house was an 18-room Italianate villa, and was named Stormfield.

This story is the longest one in the book, but also has been cut the most. The original I worked from ran to around 15,000 words and this one is about 3,500. As a single 40 minute story, this can be a challenge for both teller and audience. On the other hand, it has a very nice flow and a logical sequence of events, which makes it a natural for storytelling. With some judicious consolidation, it's not hard to find a 20-minute story in here as well.

As is typical with Twain, if you start looking for consistent structure or continuity of ideas in the original version of this story, you begin to see a lot of problems. A bit of inconsistency is one thing in a long two-part story, and quite another in a story that is presented in thirty minutes onstage. So if you go back to the original for comparison, you will see that I have not only injected some classical structure into the story, I have also eliminated some of the internal inconsistencies. In my mind, even though there's not much story structure here, this really is one of Twain's more interesting chronicles, full of insight into human nature and amusing commentary on our hopes and beliefs. I found it to be a fitting way to close out the sampling of Twain's rich legacy in this book.

EXCERPT FROM
CAPTAIN STORMFIELD'S VISIT TO HEAVEN

Adapted by Steve Daut,
Twain original first published in 1907

I don't know what I was expecting. I just figured I'd automatically end up in one of two places when I died, and most likely the warmer of the two. I never thought about the trip it would take to get there. Well, when I had been dead about thirty years I begun to get a little anxious. Mind you, I'd been whizzing through space all that time, like a comet. But it was generally pretty one-sided, because I sailed by most of them comets the same as if they were standing still. An ordinary comet don't make more than about 200,000 miles a minute. When I came across one of that sort, like Encke's and Halley's comets, for instance, it warn't anything but just a flash and a vanish, you see. One night I was swinging along at a good round gait, about a million miles a minute or more, when I flushed an uncommonly big comet about three points off my starboard bow. Well, it was so near my course that I wouldn't throw away the chance, so I fell off a point, steadied my helm, and went for him.

By and by I closed up abreast of his tail. I was like a gnat closing up on the continent of America. I had sailed along his coast for a little upwards of a hundred and fifty million miles when I could see by the shape of him that I hadn't even got up to his waistband yet. Well, I boomed along another hundred and fifty million miles, and got up abreast his shoulder, when the officer of the deck came to the side and hoisted his spyglass in my direction.

Straight off I heard him sing out, "Below there, ahoy! Shake her up, shake her up! Heave on a hundred million billion tons of brimstone!"

The race was on! In less than ten seconds that comet was just a blazing cloud of red-hot canvas. Well sir, nobody can describe the way it rolled and tumbled up into the skies, the way it smelt, or that sound of thousands of boson's whistles screaming at once. I never heard the like of it before. We roared and thundered along side by side, both doing our level best, because I'd never encountered a comet that could outrun me, so I was bound to beat this one. Well, sir, I gained and gained, little by little, till at last I went skimming sweetly by the magnificent old conflagration's nose.

By this time the captain of the comet had been rousted out, and he stood there by the mate in his shirt-sleeves and slippers, his hair all rats' nests and one suspender hanging. How sick those two men looked!

I just simply couldn't help putting my thumb to my nose as I glided away. I sang out, "Ta-ta! Ta-ta! Any word to send to your family?" I've often regretted that as a bad mistake. You see, the captain had given up the race, but that remark was too tedious for him.

He turned to the mate, and said, "Have we got brimstone enough of our own to make the trip?"

"Yes, sir."

"How much have we got in cargo for Satan?"

"Eighteen hundred thousand billion quintillions of kazarks."

"Very well, then, let his boarders freeze till the next comet comes. Lighten ship! Lively, now, lively, men! Heave the whole cargo overboard!"

Well, a kazark is exactly the bulk of a hundred and sixty-nine worlds just like ours. They hove all that load overboard. When it fell it wiped out a considerable raft of stars just as clean as if they'd been candles and somebody blowed them out.

As for the race, that was at an end. The minute she was lightened the comet swung along past me the same as if I was anchored. The captain stood on the stern, put his thumb to his nose and sung out, "Ta-ta! ta-ta! Maybe YOU'VE got some message to send your friends in the Everlasting Tropics!" Inside of an hour, his craft was only a pale torch in the distance.

Well, I got back on my course, getting lonely and uneasy again without a race to keep me occupied. But finally, one night as I was sailing along, I discovered a tremendous row of blinking lights away on the horizon ahead. As I approached, they began to tower and swell and look like mighty furnaces. I said to myself, "By George, I've arrived at last— and at the wrong place, just as I expected!" But when I got closer, I saw that the things I took for furnaces were gates, miles high, made all of flashing jewels, and they pierced a wall of solid gold that you couldn't see the top of, nor yet the end of, in either direction. I was pointed straight for one of these gates, and coming like a house afire. And the sky was black with millions of people, all heading for those gates.

I drifted up to a gate with a swarm of people and touched down. When it was my turn the head clerk said, in a business-like way, "Well, quick! Where are you from?"

"San Francisco," I said.

"Is that a planet?"

"It's a city. One of the biggest and finest in California."

"Look, there's a lot of people waiting here. System and planet, and be quick about it."

"I'm from the United States of America. Surely you know about that?"

He just waved me aside and shouted, "Next!"

Well, being an American, I was pretty indignant at being treated like that, but then I glanced around. I looked over to see a sky-blue man with seven heads and only one leg was standing there, and it occurred to me that most of the people looked a whole lot more like him than me. What's more, I didn't know a single one of them.

Well, I was puzzling through that one when a clerk came up to me and said, "We need to know what world you are from", so I said, pretty humble-like, "I'm from the world that the Savior saved."

He bent his head at the name and said gently, "The worlds He has saved are numbered like unto the gates of Heaven. No one can count them."

Well, I figured, now we were getting somewhere. Then he said, "What astronomical system is your world in? You know, what sun, moon, and planets?"

"Oh! Oh, well, uh, our planet is Earth, and there's Mars and Jupiter…"

"Jupiter! Seems to me there was a man here eight or nine years ago from that area, but people from that system almost never enter by this gate. Tell me. Did you come straight here?"

"Yes sir," I said and at that, he looked at me very stern.

"It doesn't do to lie here."

"Well," I said, "I might have raced a little with a comet one night, and got a teeny bit off course."

"Wait here," he said. "I'll try to look you up."

Well, he disappeared for a day or two, and when he got back he asked me to describe our planet and how far it is from the sun and all, and when I did, he said, "Ok, I found you, but on our map, that planet you're from is called the Wart."

At that, I wanted to say, "Young man, it wouldn't be wholesome for you to go down there and tell them that Heaven calls our precious Earth the Wart", but I kept my own counsel on that one after all the work he'd done to find the place.

Well, they let me in and told me I was safe forever and wouldn't have any more trouble. Then they went on with their work as if my case was all complete and I had disappeared from view. I marched right back up to the head clerk and demanded to know where my harp, wings, and halo were, and he said, "I don't have any idea what you're talking about. Heaven is a large place, and every kingdom has its own set of customs. I suggest you go over there and stand on the red wishing carpet. Wish your way over to Wart heaven, and you'll be there in the blink of an eye."

"Well, why didn't you tell me that before?" I said, and he replied, "We have plenty to do around here. It's your place to figure out your way around."

I stood on the carpet and wished myself to the booking office of my own section, and before I could even open my eyes, I heard a familiar voice call out, "Cap'n Eli Stormfield of San Francisco! Here's your harp, wings, and halo."

Well, I opened my eyes and sure enough, it was a Piute Indian I knew in Tulare County. He seemed right glad to see me, and I was pretty glad to see him as well, as he was one of the best men I'd ever known and a good friend. Until he died, of course. Behind him, as far as the eye could reach, was a swarm of clerks running around, tricking out millions of Yanks, Mexicans, English and Arabs, and all sorts of other kinds of people in their new outfit. "Now this is more like it, "I cried, "Point me in the direction of my cloud!"

Inside of fifteen minutes, I was a mile on my way towards the cloud-banks and about a million people along with me. We began to meet swarms of folks who were coming back from there. Some had harps, or hymn-books, or halos, and some had nothing at all. All of them looked meek and uncomfortable. One young fellow hadn't anything left but his halo, and all of a sudden he offered it to me and said, "Will you hold this for me a minute?" I took it and he disappeared in the crowd. Then I begun to see there were piles of these things floating all over the place. All these people returning from the cloud bank were dumping them right and left. But when I found myself perched on a cloud with a million other people, I never felt so good in my life. I struck in playing my harp, even though I only knew one tune.

You can't imagine the row we made, about a million of us up there on the clouds, each one playing the only tunes we knew, over and over again. It didn't take me too long to figure out why all those folks were leaving and dumping their stuff. I turned to an old man on the cloud next to me and saw that he looked about as miserable as I felt myself. I said, "I don't mean to be sacrilegious or nothing, but this ain't near to my idea of bliss as I thought it was going to be, when I used to go to church."

He said, "What do you say to knocking off and calling it half a day?" So we got out of there. We found some newcomers floating up toward the clouds and asked them to hold our stuff. They took it and we floated down far away from them, as fast as we could. We were both free men, outrageously happy to be rid of those things, but just as happy to be rid of the idea that we'd have to stay with them for all eternity.

Just then I ran across old Sam Bartlett, who had been dead a long time, and I stopped to talk to him. I commented on how this wasn't quite what I expected from church and all. He said, "Let me set you straight on that. People come up here having taken the figurative language of the Bible and the first thing they ask for is a harp and wings and so on and they get them because when you're here, you're pretty much in charge of what you want. They sit up there and sing and play, and figure out real quick that doing that for all eternity isn't a heaven that would keep a man sane for long. It sounds pretty when you hear it from the pulpit, but you'd just end up with a heaven full of warbling ignoramuses. You get to choose your occupation here, but nothing makes a thinking person happy forever. See, happiness isn't a thing in itself, it's only a contrast with something that ain't pleasant. There's plenty of pain and suffering in heaven, so there's plenty of contrasts and no end of happiness."

"Well," I said, "That's a whole lot different from the frozen wax model heaven I had in mind, but it makes a whole lot more sense."

Sam took me on as a newcomer, showing me around and learning me about heaven, and I saw that the place was full of all sorts of different kinds of people, all with different sets of looks, habits, tastes and occupations, and I realized that he was right about contrasts. It's the variation, the differences that come into pleasant collision in such a variegated society that keeps things interesting.

Just then, as if to underscore the pain and suffering he mentioned, a middle-aged woman with grizzled hair walked by. She was walking slow and droopy, with her head bent down. She was crying. Sandy said, "I've seen that look before, and it's one of the saddest things about people's heavenly expectations. That woman probably got here and found her child after pining away for it for years on earth. Say the child was two when he died, and the only comfort that woman had was that she'd see her child here in heaven and would never be parted again. But he got here and decided he didn't want to stay a child. He decided to grow and learn and keep on moving. The poor woman came in here expecting a baby to jounce, but now they're about as close company as mud and a bird o' paradise. Eventually, they'll come together and get adjusted. They got all the time in the universe."

"Seems like heaven can be a pretty disappointing place for some folks," I said.

"Well, here's the thing. There's millions of people down there on earth that are promising themselves that the first thing they are going to do when they get to heaven will be to fling their arms around Abraham, Isaac, and Jacob, and kiss them and weep on them. As many as sixty thousand people arrive here every single day who want to run straight to Abraham, Isaac and Jacob, and hug them and weep on them. Now mind you, sixty thousand a day is a pretty heavy contract for those old people. If they were a mind to allow it, they wouldn't ever have anything to do, year in and year out, but stand up and be hugged and wept on thirty-two hours in the twenty-four. They would be tired out and as wet as muskrats all the time. What would heaven be like for them? You can't accommodate everyone, no matter what the preachers like to tell you."

"See, folks down there have it pretty confused. Down there they talk of the heavenly King, but then they go right on speaking as if this was a republic and everybody was on a dead level with everybody else, and privileged to fling his arms around anybody he comes across, and be hail-fellow-well-met with all the elect, from the highest down. How tangled up and absurd that is! How are you going to have a republic under a king? How are you going to have a republic at all, where the head of the government is absolute, holds his place forever, and there ain't nobody else in the whole universe who has a voice in the government? Fine republic, ain't it?"

"But it don't matter much, because the King is a pretty fair fellow. That's the heavenly justice of it. On earth, folks aren't rewarded according to their deserts, but here they get their rightful rank. For instance, a tailor from Tennessee wrote poetry that Homer and Shakespeare couldn't begin to come up to, but nobody would print it so nobody read it but his neighbors, and they laughed at it. There was a feller from Hoboken who kept a sausage-shop and never saved a cent in his life because he used to give all his spare meat to the poor, in a quiet way. But nobody ever saw him give anything to anybody, so he had the reputation of being mean. The minute he landed here, they made him a baronet. Those who deserve it get recognized for who they are, even if they never had an opportunity on the world they came from."

"Not everyone gets a promotion, but we do our best to accommodate expectation when there's no harm in it. As long as they come through the right gate, that is." At this, he stared hard at me, and I'll have to admit it stung a bit.

He continued his thought. "For instance, there's a barkeeper that got converted at a revival meeting a little while ago, then started home on a ferry-boat, and there was a collision and he drowned. He thinks all of heaven is going to go wild with joy and have a torchlight procession for him."

I said, "I supposed he'll be disappointed, then."

Sam replied, "No he won't. We're going to have a big old to-do for him. You ought to put on your wings and come on out."

"But I left my wings up in the clouds, along with my harp and such like. I didn't think I needed them."

"You don't need them. Wings ain't for transportation. Pretty silly if you think about it, with all the distance you have to travel to get around here. No, we use wishing to travel, but the wings are a uniform for formal occasions. It's what people expect. You can go down and get some more out of inventory. And get a harp and halo to boot. It will impress that barkeep to no end."

So we got all dressed up and wished ourselves over to the reception place. The place spread out as far as the eye could see, and it was mostly empty when we first got there. But then, in the blink of an eye, it was teeming with angels, probably a hundred million of them. Well, most of them were copper colored, or reddish, or real dark brown. There wasn't even a good lecture audience of white folks. "Where's all the white ones?" I asked Sam.

"Well, it's like this," said Sam. "This is all the people who have ever lived and died in the world we come from. And through history, there's been a whole lot more of every color in the rainbow than there ever has been of white ones. So spread those white ones out over the whole sweep of it and it's like scattering a ten-cent box of homeopathic pills over the Great Sahara and expecting to find them again. You can't expect white folks to amount to much in heaven, and they don't. And white Americans are even scarcer than that. We get tourists from other planets and solar systems here, then they go back to their own section of heaven and write a travelogue and they give America about five lines in it. More often than not, they think that white folks have some terrible disease that bleached us out, due to our sinful nature. And yet we think we're going to come up here and get a hug from Abraham."

Just then, the fanfare burst out, like a million thunderstorms in one, and it made the whole heavens rock. The prodigious choir struck up and the procession began to pass, five hundred thousand angels abreast, and every angel carrying a torch and singing. The rush went on and on, then along comes the barkeeper and a great cheer went up that made the heavens shake. He was all smiles, his halo tilted over one ear in a cocky way, and he was the most satisfied-looking saint I ever saw. They walked him up to the center of the grandstand, bowing and smiling, a couple of fancied-up angels and two old men appeared out of the firmament to greet him.

Sam caught his breath at that. "Archangels!" he said. "And that's Moses and Esau!"

Well, after a bit more pomp, the crowd broke up and scattered, but Sam just kind of sat there looking shocked. When he could finally talk again, he said, "That was the most wondrous sight I've ever seen. We might go to receptions for years to come and never again see celebrities of that caliber." He said there would be a monument put up there where Moses and Esau had stood and travelers would come for thousands of years just to gawk at it and climb all over it, and scribble their names on it.

And he was right. It's like one of those rocks people paint over and over again back on earth. The barkeep comes down from the executive offices every hundred years or so, just to scrub it down.

INTRODUCTION TO

PASTOR (YOUR NAME HERE)

So I promised I'd include the story that a friend of mine said sounded like Mark Twain, and here it is. The part in this story about me being ordained by the Universal Life Church is true. The information about the church and the SafeGuard Guaranty Corporation is also true, as of this writing. Some of the other stuff is nearly true, or should be. The title of the story is meant to suggest that you can either tell it as if I told it to you, or you can steal it for your own use as long as you give me some credit for it. But if you tell it as if you are actually the ordained minister, you might want to go onto the website and get ordained (it's listed in the bibliography, or you can just "Google it"). It really is free (as of this writing, of course). And I also suggest that you double check the websites for both of the organizations that I reference, because, you know, things change.

PASTOR (YOUR NAME HERE)

by Steve Daut, 2017

"We are all children of the same universe"

This is the overarching belief of the Universal Life Church, of which I am an ordained minister. Fellow ministers include Conan O'Brien, Lady Gaga, Stephen Colbert, Richard Branson, Dwain Johnson (The Rock), Paul McCartney, and Ian McKellen. But some of the pastors in the Universal Life Church are not celebrities like us.

You become a minister in the Universal Life Church by going onto their website, picking a password, and agreeing with the core tenets. Those tenets include a couple of common sense statements about doing the right thing, and freedom of religion.

It doesn't cost a dime. Of course, if you want credentials that prove you are actually ordained, there are various packages available for various reasonable fees. I got ordained because a friend of mine was getting married, and he and his bride-to-be wanted me to perform the wedding ceremony.

As it turns out, ordination by the Universal Life Church is legal in Michigan, but the details of how to go about legally marrying people are left up to the county. I called Washtenaw County, and they told me that when I turned in the paperwork I would have to include a copy of my ordination papers, so I ordered the $39.99 wedding package from the church. Then I found out that the potentially happy couple has to apply to the county where they live, not where the ceremony is performed. They live in Wayne County, so I called the clerk's office there and they told me "Just sign the paperwork, no proof of ordination is necessary." So it became apparent that I had spent $39.99 that I didn't need to spend.

Well, we had the wedding on Halloween, which was not a big hit with the groom's evangelical family. We held the ceremony outside on a day with 28-degree wind chills, but you know, temporary inconvenience, permanent commitment. It was a very short ceremony. When I went to mail in the marriage license, I thought I'd better get a return receipt and send it next day delivery, so the marriage thing cost me another $12.75.

It didn't take long before the marriage started to get into trouble. The bride waited until their wedding night to reveal the details of her past prison experience, and when the groom told his family about it they threatened to disown him. Pretty soon, the whole thing just fell apart. So here I spent $52.74 and the darn wedding didn't even take.

I was whining to a friend about this, trying to figure out how to recoup my cost, when I realized he was an insurance agent. Marriage is a pretty risky proposition, so as kind of a joke I said that maybe instead of helping people get married I should sell marriage insurance instead. Well, he took me seriously, and he said:

"Insurance is tricky. You can lose your shirt on it if you don't do it right. What you have to do is figure out what scares the crap out of people and then convince them that you can protect them from those things. What you actually do is look at all the things that can go wrong, how much each one would cost and the likelihood that each one of those things may happen. Then you divide those things into four categories."

"The first category is things that are really likely to happen. Those become exclusions – things that you don't cover, no way, no how. For instance, you sell them hurricane insurance but exclude water and wind damage."

"Then you look at things that just might happen and you figure out how much they are worth by multiplying the amount they would cost by the likelihood that they will happen. The best opportunity is to find things that people think are going to happen a lot, but actually don't happen all that much. Then you set the premium at five times what they are worth and if they do happen you pay out half of what they cost."

"The third category is things that probably will never happen but won't cost very much if they do, and you pay on those without restriction. This proves that you actually care about your customers and they have some chance of getting some money if something terrible happens."

"The fourth group is the most important. These are the things that probably will never happen, but will cost a whopping ton of money if they ever do. You see, these are thing things that people fear the most, and so they are your best sales tool. They are what actually drive people to buy insurance in the first place, so you have to cover these, but you put so many restrictions and conditions on the payout that, from a practical standpoint, you will never have to pay anything. Say, for instance, you cover getting hit by a golf ball and becoming permanently disabled. In the fine print, you say that the ball had to be hit by a 6-iron or shorter club, the golfer had to yell 'Fore!' at least 10 seconds before the ball hit you, and you have to prove that particular golf ball never hit anyone before."

"And of course, it doesn't hurt to have a loss leader – something you sell them really cheap, or even give away for free, in order to suck them into the idea of buying insurance in the first place."

It occurred to me that if I did this right I could make a whole lot more than $40. So I went to work. I found out that divorce rates are highest in the first couple years of a marriage, and even higher for those who have been married many times before, so that fit into the first category. I decided to put in the fine print that payouts are excluded in the first two years of a marriage, and the policy was void if the total previous marriages of the two people was more than five, even if they had been paying premiums for years.

I found out that the divorce rate in America is decreasing, even though many people think it is still on the rise. That's perfect for the second group! I could charge them way more than it was worth.

I decided to make marriage free. That would be my loss leader. Of course, that meant I'd lose $12.75 in mailing costs every time I did a wedding, so I had to pitch the insurance thing hard to break even. I figured that while I'm doing the pre-marriage conference I'd mention how risky it was to get married. We'd discuss the idea of divorce and when they got cold feet, Wham!, I'd sell them the divorce insurance.

And I'd have all different kinds of insurance. They could buy a term marriage policy for, say, five years, but they would pay really high premiums for that. Then I'd have whole life marriage insurance, with much lower premiums. I'd tell them the whole life option would be best, even though they had to pay for it forever. But I would be telling the truth, because it really would be the best value for me.

So I put an ad in the paper, offering my free marriage services. I sat down with my first potentially happy couple and went over all the options. I guess I got a little carried away because at the end they decided it was too risky, so they didn't want to get married after all.

I went back to the drawing board. I added a conversion option in the policy to convert their marriage to dual lifetime memberships in my new online dating site. With the next couple that came in, when I got to the insurance part the couple told me they already had divorce insurance through SafeGuard Guaranty Corporation. You can look it up. They even have an online divorce probability calculator! You put in all this personal information and it calculates the likelihood that you'll get divorced. They say it has an estimated 87% accuracy rate!

So I have some competition in that space. I'm not giving up. I went back to the drawing board and came up with a new business model. If you know anyone who wants to get married, or you would like to renew your vows at no cost, give me a call. Your only obligation is to sit through a 90-minute presentation in which I explain the many benefits of time-share marriage. It's really a good deal. A whole year lease will only cost you $39.99, plus $12.75 shipping and handling. Anybody?

BIBLIOGRAPHY

Andrews, Evan, "The Cardiff Giant Fools the Nation, 145 Years Ago", http://www.history.com/news/the-cardiff-giant-fools-the-nation-145-years-ago

Kuhn, Thomas s., Ian Hacking. *The Structure of Scientific Revolutions*, London: University of Chicago Press, 2012.

Library of Congress newspapers, https://www.loc.gov/newspapers/

Lyle, Cy ed., "Journalism in Tennessee", *The Comet*, March 17,1888, 1.

"Mark Twain in The Californian 1864-1867", http://www.twain-quotes.com/Calif/califindex.html

Marvin's Marvelous Mechanical Museum, http://www.marvin3m.com/

Naparsteck, Martin, Michele Cardulla. *Mrs. Mark Twain: The Life of Olivia Langdon Clemens*, 1845-1904, Jefferson, NC: McFarland & Company, 2014.

Paine, Albert Bigelow, "Fresh Findings From Mark Twain", *San Francisco Call*, February 16, 1913, 4.

Paine, Albert B., "Thirteen New Stories of Mark Twain", *The Washington Herald*, December 17, 1916, 14.

Reigstad, Thomas J. *Scribblin' For a Livin'*, New York, NY: Prometheus Books, 2013.

"Scene on the Ajax", *Belmont Chronicle*, May 10, 1865, 1.

Safeguard Guaranty Corporation, http://www.safeguardguaranty.com/

Stead, Phillip, Mark Twain, Erin Stead (illustrator). *The Purloining of Prince Oleomargarine*, New York, NY: Random House Children's Books, 2017.

The Cardiff Giant, http://www.hoaxes.org/archive/permalink/the_cardiff_giant/

Trout, Carolyn, "Samuel Langhorne Clemens", *State Historical Society of Missouri*, https://www.shsmo.org/historicmissourians/name/c/clemens/#intro

Twain, Mark, "A Humorous View of the Farmer's Club", *Belmont Chronicle*, December 15,1870, 4.

Twain, Mark, "Arguing With a Raven", *Cincinnati Daily Star*, May 18,1880, 6.

Twain, Mark, "Curing a Cold", *Marshall County Republican*, May 24, 1867, 1.

Twain, Mark. *Life on the Mississippi*, Boston, MA: James R. Osgood and Company, 1883.

Twain, Mark, "Mark Twain as an Agricultural Editor", *The Democratic Press*, December 8,1870, 4.

Twain, Mark. *Mark Twain's Sketches, New and Old*, Hartford, CT: American Publishing Company, 1882.

Twain, Mark, "Mental Telegraphy", *The New York Daily Tribune*, November 29, 1891, 14.

Twain, Mark, "New Hotel", *Evening Star*, November 5,1881, 2.

Twain, Mark. *The Man That Corrupted Hadleyburg, and Other Stories and Essays*, New York NY: Harper & Brothers, 1900

Twain, Mark, "The Private Habits of Greeley", *The Fremont Weekly Journal*, June 14, 1872, 1.

Twain, Mark. *What is Man? And Other Essays*, New York, Harper and Brothers: 1906.

Twain, Mark, Albert Bigelow Paine, (editor). *Mark Twain's Autobiography*, New York, NY: Harper and Brothers, 1924.

Twain, Mark, E.W. Kemble (illustrator). *Mark Twain's Library of Humor*, Picadilly, London: Chatto & Windus, 1888.

Twain, Mark, John Paul (editor). *The Celebrated Jumping Frog of Calaveras County, and Other Sketches*, New York, NY: C.H. Webb, 1867.

Twain, Mark, Joseph B. McCullough, Janice McIntire-Strasburg (editors). *Mark Twain at the Buffalo Express*, DeKalb, IL: Northern Illinois University Press, 1999

Universal Life Church, https://www.themonastery.org/

"What Mark Twain Said", *New York Daily Tribune*, December 23, 1882, 2.

AUTHOR BIOGRAPHY

Steve Daut has been telling stories ever since the dog ate his homework. A performer for 35 years, his onstage credits include magic shows, stand-up comedy, improv, and storytelling. Daut's program, *Telling Twain*, has been accepted for inclusion in the 2018-2021 Michigan Arts and Humanities Touring Directory.

Author of *Buddha Science* (nonfiction), Steve is trained and experienced as a scientist, and he also has worked in the non-profit sector. He is a member of the National Storytelling Network and president of the Ann Arbor Storytellers Guild. He is a graduate of the Second City and the Purple Rose Theatre Actor-Director Lab. Currently, he is devoted full time to writing and storytelling. Personal pursuits include pickleball, golf, and throwing a flying disk for his incessantly insistent dog, Rose.

Steve has led discussion groups and conducted training sessions for technical educators, nonprofits, governmental organizations, and college-level coursework at Southern Michigan prison. He has helped to facilitate community sessions and has presented day-long storytelling retreats as well as shorter storytelling workshops.

Steve's versatile, improvisational storytelling style engages a wide variety of audiences. A typical show for adults includes personal stories from heartwarming to hilarious, some bits of humorous history, and perhaps a Mark Twain story or two. He brings quirky characters to stage, often finding wisdom in the most unlikely places. His shows for younger children involve traditional folk tales, a lot of interaction, and a touch of magic.

AUTHOR Q&A

With Steve Daut

1. When did you start telling stories?

I like to say I have been telling stories ever since my dog first ate my homework. There were family problems when I was young, and I think like many other kids I acted goofy and told stories as a way of dealing with difficult issues. I grew up as something of a class ham, and I used to do magic shows for the neighborhood kids in my backyard.

2. You have written plays. You have performed stage magic, improv, standup comedy, and of course storytelling. Can you talk about the similarities and differences between these forms?

Plays keep what they call the fourth wall in place. The world of the play is self-contained, and the audience is drawn into it. The other four break down that fourth wall, and so they are more interactive. Improv and standup tend to be more spontaneous and interactive, but less structured, while storytelling as a form can have some improvisational elements, but it shares the structural elements with plays, in that a story has a distinct beginning, middle, and end.

3. Why did you settle on the form of storytelling?

Well, I have fun with magic, but it's very equipment intensive. You are always lugging stuff around, and I got tired of that. And I like to be more involved with an audience than is possible with plays, so I tried the comedy forms. I like to say that if storytelling is like weed, then standup is crack cocaine. It's a very intense experience, but because of the types of audience you get, there is a tendency to get raunchy, and I didn't like that aspect of it. The moment I stepped onstage as a storyteller, I knew I had found my niche. The audiences are very supportive, and you can tell stories that touch on important truths.

4. Would you say you have a storytelling style? Something specific you like to do in your stories?

I like to inhabit the characters. I tend to tell stories about finding wisdom in unusual places. I have met some people who the world would consider failures, or at least those who are down and out, and I have learned some profound lessons from them. There is great wisdom in people who have struggled to get through life.

5. What makes a story interesting to you?

I love to find and tell stories that present a mix of funniness and seriousness. Quirky characters, silly or unusual ways of looking at things, unexpected twists and turns in a story are always good. But they also need to have some underlying lesson, that universal truth that people can connect to at the deepest levels. If I can make people want to laugh and cry at the same time, that's a good story. Oh, and I like ending with a twist.

6. Why Mark Twain?

Well, he has a lot of the elements that I like in a story, and I find it natural to settle into a folksy character with a slight drawl, the kind of character that Twain often uses as his narrator. I also have found his stories to be a lot farther ranging than a lot of people give him credit for, so it's fun to tell a story and people are surprised that it's something that Twain wrote.

7. Some people consider it almost sacrilegious to change Mark Twain's stories, but you rewrite them all the time. Tell me about that.

A lot of Twain's stories deal with universal themes and are just as relevant today as they were in his day. But they can get bogged down in the vernacular of 150 years ago, and some of them are pretty wordy because he often padded his stories to fill column space in newspapers. So people come to view Mark Twain stories as historical, and they lose the current relevance. I try to modernize them just enough that people get past the historical part and see how germane the stories still are today.

8. You say your life parallels Twain's in many ways. Can you explain?

Well, Twain was born in Florida, Missouri and grew up in Hannibal, so he was a river rat. I was born in Davenport Iowa, and moved to Muscatine, also on the Mississippi River. He lost his father at age 12, and mine was lost to me when I was seven. And although I have made my living in a more conventional way, writing and publishing, and being on stage has been a constant in my life, as it was for Twain.

9. What was it like growing up without a father?

Well, my father didn't die like Twain's did. Instead, my parents divorced when I was seven, and I only saw my dad sporadically after that. I like to say that because I lacked a father to learn about the world, I became a Ray Bradbury Martian, absorbing the experiences and personas of those around me. That may be true of every kid, but it was especially true for me. We moved to a new town, right next door to my grandparents and my grandfather became a default dad for me.

10. Tell us about your grandfather.

He was an old German guy with a bent leg and a twinkle in his eye. He had broken his leg seven times when he was a kid, and by the time I knew him, he had to walk with a crutch, but he didn't let that stop him. But he had a great sense of humor and a sweet disposition. He would tease my grandmother endlessly and wink at me when she got frustrated with him. For years, I thought he had a pet name for me. What he showed me how to do something, I thought he was saying "See, Stu?" Later on, I discovered that he was saying, "Siehst du?", which is German for "You see?" He gave me an onion once for a birthday present. One Thanksgiving dinner when I asked him to pass the cookie plate, he dumped the cookies on the table and handed me the plate.

11. Later in life, you reconnected with your father. How did that go?

He had been diagnosed with advanced pancreatic cancer a couple of months earlier, and at the time I think the life expectancy at diagnosis was something like three weeks. I got a call from my brother that he was asking for me, and there was no time left, but I postponed it as long as I could. I had ignored him most of my life, and I just didn't want to deal with him. Finally, I ran out of excuses and went to see him. I sat and talked with him for hours. When we started that conversation, we were strangers, but by the time I left, we were father and son. I left, and 24 hours later, he was dead. He had been waiting for me, and as soon as we reconciled, he let go.

AUTHOR'S ESSAY

by Steve Daut

I was born in Davenport Iowa and raised in nearby Muscatine, Iowa, both towns on the Mississippi River that was so much a part of Mark Twain's early stories. I remember frequent trips to Hannibal, Missouri, to visit Twain's childhood home and ride the Delta Queen, a restored historic riverboat that was a tourist favorite. My mother read Mark Twain stories to me from my early youth, and I loved to imagine Jim Smiley and that notorious frog, Tom and Huck just hanging out on the river, and cruising down the river with rough-and-tumble riverboat gamblers. The gambler's life continued to grow in my imagination as I watched episodes of Brett Maverick outwitting everyone around him with a wink and a smile.

I had something of a Tom Sawyer childhood myself, hanging out down by the river. Right in downtown Muscatine, there was a big parking lot that sloped down into the river, with a building on one end that had an abutment that stood probably three feet out above the water, and we used to ride our bikes off that abutment, flying out into mid-air for a moment, then plunging into the cool river water. Then we would drag our bikes out of the water and do it over and over again. I also remember summer days at a little cottage on the river, and frequent paddle trips out to a little sandy island full of mosquitoes, rotting logs, and the fattest frogs a kid could ever hope to find.

Today, Twain's stories not only take me back to that time but in taking a closer look at the humanity and the insight in them, I begin to realize how connected we are, not only today but through time. When I read *The McWilliamses and the Burglar Alarm*, I think about experiences I have had calling for technical help with my computer. When I read *Journalism in Tennessee*, I am reminded of our current obsession with "fake news." The more I read, study, and tell Mark Twain stories, the more convinced I am of the importance of hearing his voice today.

As a storyteller, I look for the universal story underneath the specific physical facts of a tale. Twain was in touch with the universal. His stories speak to our deepest impulses. Twain crafted his tales in ways that help us look closely at those impulses and laugh at ourselves at the same time. When I tell any story, whether it's a personal story, a folktale, or an original Twain story, I feel most successful if I can make people feel like laughing and crying *at the same time.* Twain mixes social observation with personal insight and political commentary in a way we have lost, and we would do well to get back. We need perspective on what has led us to the polarized world we live in today. But too often, when we look at Twain's stories, his oversized persona gets in the way of the stories he has to tell. Like watching a Sylvester Stallone movie, if there is a plot involved, it gets subsumed under the towering image of the character he plays. If we can avoid getting caught up in the vernacular of the time, and the image of that white suit and string tie, we can begin to see the universal in these stories. That's why I wanted to adapt these stories for a modern audience.

But it's not only the stories that are compelling for me. It is the true story of the man named Samuel Langhorne Clemens, a man who rose from humble beginnings, found his passion early in life, and, through hard work and persistence, was fortunate enough to make a living doing what he loved. It is also the story of a man who knew struggle, who fell into debt early in life, whose eternal optimism drew him to invest over and over again in risky business deals and who consequently spent much his hard-earned money in paying off debts. International copyright laws were notoriously weak when Twain started publishing his works, and many volumes were published overseas that netted Twain no income at all. In the U.S, copyright terms were limited to 14 years, with one extension, but even here and in Canada, unscrupulous publishers would routinely pirate his works.

As time went on, Clemens became a staunch advocate for extended copyright protection. He testified at the British House of Lords and the United States Congress, initially advocating for copyright protection "in perpetuity," but later settling on the author's life and fifty years after. His wish was not granted until 1976. Clemens' attitude toward copyright was summed up in one laugh-line: "Only one thing is impossible for God: To find any sense in any copyright law on the planet."

Because I work with Twain stories, I think a lot about copyright. According to the United States Copyright office, anything first published in the U.S. before 1923 is in the public domain, and the most recent story in *Telling Twain* was first published in 1907. But there is a legal side of these things and a moral side of them, as well.

In one of the stories I tell (not a Mark Twain story), I start with a few lyrics from a song, and though by any stretch of the imagination, the way I do it is "fair use," I decided to make efforts to contact the lyricist, not only to seek his blessing, but to let him know how his beautiful words affected my life. Sadly, he sounded weary of the praise, possibly the way Clemmons might have sounded late in his life. He told me that the words had nothing to do with him anymore, as the record company claimed the right to them. Perhaps the record company was exercising a legal right, but it seems like moral vampirism to take a man's words while he is still alive. Now, 155 years after a story was first published under the pseudonym Mark Twain, I just hope that the way I tell his stories, and my reimagining of them, would have brought a smile and a nod of approval to the man who wrote the original versions. I have done my best to make it so.

Samuel Clemens was born in Florida, Missouri, in 1835. His family struggled financially, and he was only twelve when he began working to help his family. In his first jobs, he worked for newspapers at menial tasks: running errands, delivering papers, setting type. When he was twelve, he lost his father. These things echoed through my life as well.

Although my father didn't die when I was young, he left my life when I was seven. I was fortunate in that I found many wonderful men who supported me. In particular, my grandfather became a steady and supportive presence in my life. An old German with a twinkle in his eye, he always had a joke and a story for me, and he certainly contributed to my enjoyment of Mark Twain, as he shared Twain's ability to laugh through the trials of life. He developed my sense of humor early, and my ability to laugh at myself, such as when he gave me an onion for a birthday present, and when at a big Thanksgiving dinner I asked him to pass the cookie plate, he proceeded to dump the cookies on the table and hand me the plate.

Like Twain, I also had early experience with printing. I used to help a friend's father put together the newsletter for our church, setting lead type into trays to load onto his little printing press. Later, in one of my first jobs, I would strip type and photos into masking sheets to burn plates for the more modern offset presses at a small print shop.

Around age 27, Clemens began to get writing assignments, producing serious reports and humorous articles for the *Virginia City Territorial Enterprise*. In 1863, he began using the pseudonym Mark Twain, a river term that means "two fathoms deep." After *Jim Smiley and His Jumping Frog* was published in the *New York Saturday Press* (1865), Twain became a household name, a name interchangeable with Clemens for the rest of his life. He spent much of his life lecturing, speaking, and reading to promote his many books and publications.

Although I made my living in more traditional ways, writing and performing have always been a part of my life. When I was young, I would perform backyard magic shows for the neighborhood. I performed close-up and stage magic off and on until my 40's. Following the advice of Harlan Ellison, I have written more than million words in my lifetime, a reasonable fraction of it for publication. In seventh grade, I wrote a humor column for our class newspaper, and I have written humor columns for at least four publications since then, under various pseudonyms. I have actually lost track of the number of times my work has been published, but it runs in the hundreds. And I have performed for years as an MC, in comedy sketches and a play or two, as a standup comedian, an MC, and of course, as a storyteller. Today, writing and storytelling is what I do. I feel incredibly privileged that I am able to follow this passion, and walk in the shoes of Mark Twain.

Onstage, I try to mix up my storytelling with personal stories, traditional tales, and a bit of Mark Twain. My goal is to serve the story and the audience rather than creating a "Mark Twain character". Although I develop and perform shows for very young children, I am more focused on older children and adults, who can understand a story at many levels. It seems to me that we should be able to take ourselves and our travails seriously without taking them soberly. Although everyone likes to laugh, life can also deliver pain and disappointment, and stories not only reflect life, but they can teach us how to live it. As Twain writes in *Excerpt From Captain Stormfield's Visit to Heaven*, "See, happiness isn't a thing in itself, it's only a contrast with something that ain't pleasant. There's plenty of pain and suffering in heaven, so there's plenty of contrasts and no end of happiness."

Each story in this book, and each story I tell has a unique purpose. My goal in sharing these stories, both in the oral and written form, is to provide a variety of thoughts and ideas, and also unique perspectives on the way we relate to each other and the events that create our world. Sometimes the goal may just be to laugh, other times it may be to mourn, to be disgusted or exuberant or satisfied. Sometimes it is all of these things. But I always try to select the mix of stories to avoid formula, to not only mix up styles and topics, but story and sentence structure as well. Each story should be a new and unexpected experience, loaded with surprise and unpredictability. If I am successful in a storytelling event, or in *Telling Twain*, it is because my audience is constantly asking themselves, "My God, what is he going to say next?" That, for me, is the appeal of Mark Twain. His stories are a darn site deeper than two fathoms, and they are as wide as the ocean. And always, always, they are full of good humor and humanity. They may poke fun at others, but they also poke fun right back at the narrator.

Ironically, although *Telling Twain* is all about work written under the pseudonym of Mark Twain, at another level it's not really about the persona that Samuel Clemens created at all. It is about recognizing a vast storehouse of wonderful stories that is in the public domain and accessible to us, but that we don't always recognize because it is often buried underneath a larger-than-life historical character. Recognition of the buried legacy of stories is the same reason that many of us storytellers focus on folk tales or fairy tales, or tales from one particular tradition or culture. As with Mark Twain, any good story connects us. The audience members may not be able to relate to the specific physical circumstances of a story. They may never have attended a frog jumping contest or run for political office, but they certainly can relate to a couple of men getting into a test of egos, or politicians arguing over which one is telling the truth and which one is spouting "fake news". More broadly, we can all relate to the absurdity of arguing about trivial matters and frustration at not having a solid, unwavering truth that we can rely upon, or someone to reliably deliver that truth. It is the story underneath the story that compels us to listen to yet one more story. I hope that you, as a reader or teller of these stories, will connect with them as deeply as I do. After all, we are all just trying to learn about the mystery that surrounds us.

As you or I tell or read these stories, when everyone laughs at the same moment, or when we see a light of recognition or a little nod from someone in the audience, it's a physical sign that a connection has been made. And when we make those connections, we all discover, once again, that we are all in this together. And we are, all in this together. We need to know that, now more than ever. I hope you will experience those moments of connection the way I have, and that your life is made richer because of them. That is the gift these stories can give us, and it is the reason that *Telling Twain* exists.